T0080203

Intelligence: A Very Short Introduction

VERY SHORT INTRODUCTIONS are for anyone wanting a stimulating and accessible way into a new subject. They are written by experts, and have been translated into more than 45 different languages.

The series began in 1995, and now covers a wide variety of topics in every discipline. The VSI library currently contains over 600 volumes—a Very Short Introduction to everything from Psychology and Philosophy of Science to American History and Relativity—and continues to grow in every subject area.

Very Short Introductions available now:

ABOLITIONISM Richard S. Newman
THE ABRAHAMIC RELIGIONS
    Charles L. Cohen
ACCOUNTING Christopher Nobes
ADAM SMITH Christopher J. Berry
ADOLESCENCE Peter K. Smith
ADVERTISING Winston Fletcher
AERIAL WARFARE Frank Ledwidge
AESTHETICS Bence Nanay
AFRICAN AMERICAN RELIGION
    Eddie S. Glaude Jr
AFRICAN HISTORY John Parker
    and Richard Rathbone
AFRICAN POLITICS Ian Taylor
AFRICAN RELIGIONS
    Jacob K. Olupona
AGEING Nancy A. Pachana
AGNOSTICISM Robin Le Poidevin
AGRICULTURE Paul Brassley
    and Richard Soffe
ALBERT CAMUS Oliver Gloag
ALEXANDER THE GREAT
    Hugh Bowden
ALGEBRA Peter M. Higgins
AMERICAN CULTURAL HISTORY
    Eric Avila
AMERICAN FOREIGN RELATIONS
    Andrew Preston
AMERICAN HISTORY Paul S. Boyer
AMERICAN IMMIGRATION
    David A. Gerber
AMERICAN LEGAL HISTORY
    G. Edward White
AMERICAN NAVAL HISTORY
    Craig L. Symonds

AMERICAN POLITICAL HISTORY
    Donald Critchlow
AMERICAN POLITICAL PARTIES
    AND ELECTIONS L. Sandy Maisel
AMERICAN POLITICS
    Richard M. Valelly
THE AMERICAN PRESIDENCY
    Charles O. Jones
THE AMERICAN REVOLUTION
    Robert J. Allison
AMERICAN SLAVERY
    Heather Andrea Williams
THE AMERICAN WEST
    Stephen Aron
AMERICAN WOMEN'S HISTORY
    Susan Ware
ANAESTHESIA Aidan O'Donnell
ANALYTIC PHILOSOPHY
    Michael Beaney
ANARCHISM Colin Ward
ANCIENT ASSYRIA Karen Radner
ANCIENT EGYPT Ian Shaw
ANCIENT EGYPTIAN ART AND
    ARCHITECTURE Christina Riggs
ANCIENT GREECE Paul Cartledge
THE ANCIENT NEAR EAST
    Amanda H. Podany
ANCIENT PHILOSOPHY Julia Annas
ANCIENT WARFARE
    Harry Sidebottom
ANGELS David Albert Jones
ANGLICANISM Mark Chapman
THE ANGLO-SAXON AGE John Blair
ANIMAL BEHAVIOUR
    Tristram D. Wyatt

THEATRE Marvin Carlson
THEOLOGY David F. Ford
THINKING AND REASONING
    Jonathan St B. T. Evans
THOMAS AQUINAS Fergus Kerr
THOUGHT Tim Bayne
TIBETAN BUDDHISM
    Matthew T. Kapstein
TIDES David George Bowers and
    Emyr Martyn Roberts
TOCQUEVILLE Harvey C. Mansfield
TOPOLOGY Richard Earl
TRAGEDY Adrian Poole
TRANSLATION Matthew Reynolds
THE TREATY OF VERSAILLES
    Michael S. Neiberg
TRIGONOMETRY
    Glen Van Brummelen
THE TROJAN WAR Eric H. Cline
TRUST Katherine Hawley
THE TUDORS John Guy
TWENTIETH-CENTURY BRITAIN
    Kenneth O. Morgan
TYPOGRAPHY Paul Luna
THE UNITED NATIONS
    Jussi M. Hanhimäki
UNIVERSITIES AND COLLEGES
    David Palfreyman and Paul Temple
THE U.S. CONGRESS
    Donald A. Ritchie

THE U.S. CONSTITUTION
    David J. Bodenhamer
THE U.S. SUPREME COURT
    Linda Greenhouse
UTILITARIANISM
    Katarzyna de Lazari-Radek and
    Peter Singer
UTOPIANISM Lyman Tower Sargent
VETERINARY SCIENCE James Yeates
THE VIKINGS Julian D. Richards
VIRUSES Dorothy H. Crawford
VOLTAIRE Nicholas Cronk
WAR AND TECHNOLOGY
    Alex Roland
WATER John Finney
WAVES Mike Goldsmith
WEATHER Storm Dunlop
THE WELFARE STATE David Garland
WILLIAM SHAKESPEARE
    Stanley Wells
WITCHCRAFT Malcolm Gaskill
WITTGENSTEIN A. C. Grayling
WORK Stephen Fineman
WORLD MUSIC Philip Bohlman
THE WORLD TRADE
    ORGANIZATION Amrita Narlikar
WORLD WAR II Gerhard L. Weinberg
WRITING AND SCRIPT
    Andrew Robinson
ZIONISM Michael Stanislawski

Available soon:

SMELL Matthew Cobb
THE SUN Philip Judge
DEMENTIA Kathleen Taylor

NUMBER THEORY
    Robin Wilson
FIRE Andrew C. Scott

For more information visit our website

www.oup.com/vsi/

Ian J. Deary

INTELLIGENCE

A Very Short Introduction

SECOND EDITION

OXFORD
UNIVERSITY PRESS

OXFORD

UNIVERSITY PRESS

Great Clarendon Street, Oxford, OX2 6DP,
United Kingdom

Oxford University Press is a department of the University of Oxford.
It furthers the University's objective of excellence in research, scholarship,
and education by publishing worldwide. Oxford is a registered trade mark of
Oxford University Press in the UK and in certain other countries

© Ian J. Deary 2020

The moral rights of the author have been asserted

First edition published 2001
Second edition published 2020

Impression: 4

All rights reserved. No part of this publication may be reproduced, stored in
a retrieval system, or transmitted, in any form or by any means, without the
prior permission in writing of Oxford University Press, or as expressly permitted
by law, by licence or under terms agreed with the appropriate reprographics
rights organization. Enquiries concerning reproduction outside the scope of the
above should be sent to the Rights Department, Oxford University Press, at the
address above

You must not circulate this work in any other form
and you must impose this same condition on any acquirer

Published in the United States of America by Oxford University Press
198 Madison Avenue, New York, NY 10016, United States of America

British Library Cataloguing in Publication Data
Data available

Library of Congress Control Number: 2019957849

ISBN 978-0-19-879620-6

Printed in Great Britain by
Ashford Colour Press Ltd, Gosport, Hampshire

Links to third party websites are provided by Oxford in good faith and
for information only. Oxford disclaims any responsibility for the materials
contained in any third party website referenced in this work.

Contents

Preface and acknowledgements

People value their powers of thinking. Most of us are interested in why some people appear to be brighter than others. Differences between people in their broad powers of intelligence have been recognized since antiquity. Our language has many words that signify the possession or lack of the general ability to think well. In academic psychology, there is a section of researchers and teachers called 'differential psychologists'. I am one of them. We study the differences between people in intelligence and personality. In this short book, I describe some of the things that we have discovered about how and why people differ in their thinking powers. The intent, method, and style of my first edition remain, even though most of this book is new. I still think that the best way to begin to learn about people's intelligence differences is to read about specific, high-quality studies in the field. I attempt to cut out the middle person and put you in touch with some actual research data in human intelligence.

I have not tried to cover every aspect of intelligence research. The *Very Short Introduction* format is too brief for that. However, I have addressed ten areas that I think are important. I have styled them as questions which form the titles of the chapters. I think people will want to know the answers to them. The ten topics I chose accord well with the American Psychological Association's broad survey of intelligence (discussed in Chapter 10). My focus on intelligence test scores is the approach recognized by Nisbett et al.'s wide survey as the main research approach to people's intelligence differences (also in Chapter 10). Within each of my ten topics, I aim to present individual studies with ungainsayably strong data, and reliable meta-analyses. If you get into an argument about intelligence on any of these important topics, the studies I discussed will cover your back.

For each of the ten chosen areas of intelligence, I illustrate some key findings with a few individual studies. Quite often, those studies come from my team's research. I stress that these are not the only studies available. All my example studies are chosen because they have good data and they reflect the general findings of the field of research. Where there are different interpretations of those areas, I point out some further reading. Suggested further reading also takes you to other studies in those ten areas, and into fields of intelligence research that I have not had the space to cover. The Further Reading section and Chapter 10 also address some of the historical and recent controversies in intelligence research.

Most of this second edition is new. I am grateful to colleagues, friends, family, and renowned scholars (some belong to more than one category) who made good suggestions after reading my draft chapters. I thank Drew Altschul, Janie Corley, Simon Cox, Gail Davies, Ann Deary, Matthew Deary, Douglas Detterman, Morna Dewar, Chloe Fawns-Ritchie, James Flynn, Catharine Gale, Richard Haier, Sarah Harris, Caroline Hayward, Matthew Iveson, Joanna Kendall, David Lubinski, Michelle Luciano, Judy Okely, Lindsay Paterson, Stuart Ritchie, Timothy Salthouse, Adele Taylor, Philip A. Vernon, and Elayne Williamson. I thank Danielle Page for helping with proofreading. I thank Jenny Nugee and Latha Menon at Oxford University Press.

As I did in the first edition, I wrote, here, for my mum, Isobelle. She does not accept a statement without finding out where it came from. I commend her example. I hope that the illustrative data sets herein, and my descriptions and explanations of them, can bear her and your intelligent scrutiny. The chapters here use the ten topics that I present in my lay talks on intelligence. I call them 'Ten quite interesting things about intelligence'. I hope they are.

Note for the reader: I shall often refer to correlations and the sizes of correlations. If you are not sure what a correlation is, I explain it in an Appendix at the end. I recommend that you read that before starting Chapter 1. I also explain, there, what a meta-analysis is; I'll describe many of those.

List of illustrations

Chapter 1
Is there one intelligence or many?

Comments on people's mental abilities are a commonplace. Yet, when we call people 'clever', 'smart', 'intelligent', 'bright', or 'sharp', there can be an ambiguity. On the one hand, we are sometimes referring to people as being generally mentally able or less so: 'What a bright girl!' Contrariwise, we sometimes pick out a special mental ability that a person has in abundance, and that appears to contrast with their otherwise modest arrangements: 'He's good with figures, but he can never remember where he puts things, and he has no common sense.' In this first chapter, we find out whether some people are generally clever or not.

What I shall do next is give a description of the sorts of things measured in a well-known and widely used set of intelligence tests. I then ask whether these different skills are related to each other, or whether they are distinct. As I describe the set mental tests, keep in mind the question: 'If a person is good at this mental task, are they likely to be good at the others too?'

The Wechsler Adult Intelligence Scale IV

The first research story here concerns the decision by a large international psychological testing company to update its most comprehensive intelligence test battery for adults. They tested over 2,000 people. Using this dataset, the question I want to address is: do people tend to be good at some mental tests and poor at others, or are people just generally good or bad at mental tests? By mental tests, I mean cognitive tests; tests that assess people's thinking skills.

Figure 1 lists the mental tasks that people were asked to do in this dataset. There are fifteen rectangular boxes at the bottom of the diagram. Each of these boxes has the name of a different mental test. The fifteen tests make up the collection of tests called the Wechsler Adult Intelligence Scale, version IV. This is shortened to WAIS-IV. It costs many hundreds of dollars or pounds to buy. It may only be bought by people with the proper credentials, for example, educational, clinical, and occupational psychologists. It may be administered only by a trained psychological tester, working one to one with the person being tested for up to a couple of hours. The fifteen individual tests involve a wide range of mental effort for the person being tested. It is useful to describe the individual tests and some of the items so that we are not discussing this topic abstractly. This means that, for the rest of the book, it will be clear which sorts of thinking tests people have taken when they get good, average, or poor scores on intelligence tests. Because the tests are copyrighted, I describe items that are similar to those that appear in the Wechsler test battery, but not any actual items themselves. There are many other sets of mental tests. I chose the WAIS because it is so widely used and has been going for so long. If I had chosen another set, the results would have been similar. In subsequent chapters, we shall read about many other individual intelligence tests and test batteries.

If a person were to sit the WAIS-IV test, here's what they would do. I name the fifteen subtests, and I describe each one briefly. I state how many items each test contains.

Similarities. Say what two words have in common. For example: In what way are an apple and a pear alike? In what way are a painting and a symphony alike? (18 questions)

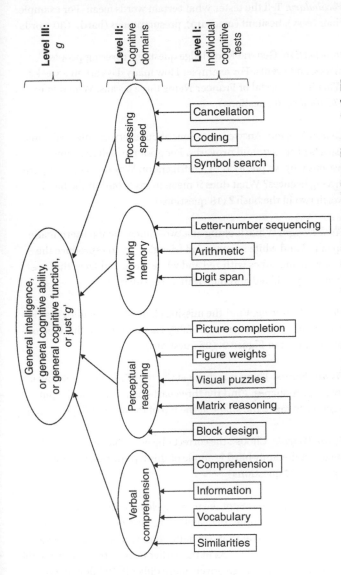

1. The three-level hierarchy of mental ability test scores from the Wechsler Adult Intelligence Scale IV.

Level III: *g*

General intelligence, or general cognitive ability, or general cognitive function, or just '*g*'

Level II: Cognitive domains

- Processing speed
- Working memory
- Perceptual reasoning
- Verbal comprehension

Level I: Individual cognitive tests

Processing speed
- Cancellation
- Coding
- Symbol search

Working memory
- Letter-number sequencing
- Arithmetic
- Digit span

Perceptual reasoning
- Picture completion
- Figure weights
- Visual puzzles
- Matrix reasoning
- Block design

Verbal comprehension
- Comprehension
- Information
- Vocabulary
- Similarities

Vocabulary. Tell the tester what certain words mean. For example: chair (easy), hesitant (medium), presumptuous (hard). (30 words)

Information. General knowledge questions covering people, places, and events. For example: How many days are in a week? What is the capital of France? Name three oceans. Who wrote *The Iliad*? (26 questions)

Comprehension. Answer questions about everyday-life problems, aspects of society, and proverbs. For example: Tell me some reasons why we put food in a refrigerator. Why do people require driving licences? What does it mean to say 'a bird in the hand is worth two in the bush'? (18 questions)

Block Design. While looking at a two-dimensional pattern made up of red and white squares and triangles, try to reproduce the pattern using cubes with red and white faces, and faces that are diagonally half-red and half-white. (14 patterns)

Matrix Reasoning. Find the missing element in a pattern that is built up in a logical manner. A fairly easy example of this type of task is shown in Figure 2. (26 questions)

Visual Puzzles. There is a shape at the top of each page. Below it are six part-shapes. Find the three part-shapes that can be put together to make the shape at the top of the page. (26 questions)

Figure Weights. Choose the correct objects to balance a scale in weight. A medium-hard example of this type of task is shown in Figure 3. (27 questions)

Picture Completion. Spot the missing element in a series of colour drawings. For example: that spokes are missing from one wheel in a picture of a bicycle; that one buttonhole is missing from a jacket in a picture of a person. As in the earlier tests in the collection, the questions become progressively more difficult. (24 drawings)

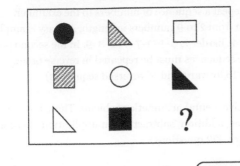

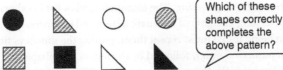

> Which of these shapes correctly completes the above pattern?

2. An example of a matrix reasoning item. This was not taken from the Wechsler Adult Intelligence Scale IV because their test materials are protected by copyright. It is an item developed for, but not used in, the revision of the Raven's Progressive Matrices intelligence test.

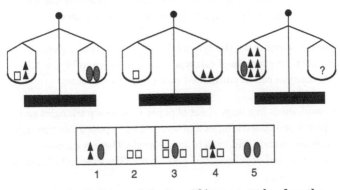

3. An example of a figure weights item. This was not taken from the Wechsler Adult Intelligence Scale IV because their test materials are protected by copyright. I have constructed this item to be similar to the sort of item that appears in the test. This item is not very easy. Which of the five possible responses is correct, so that the third scale will be balanced?

Digit Span. Repeat a sequence of numbers to the examiner. Sequences run from 2 to 9 numbers in length. An easy example is to repeat 3–7–4; harder is 3–9–1–7–4–5–3–9. In the second part of this test the sequences must be repeated in reverse order. (Maximum of 16 forward and 16 reversed sequences)

Arithmetic. Solve mental arithmetic problems. These involve simple counting, addition, subtraction, multiplication, division, and percentages. (22 questions)

Letter–number Sequencing. The examiner reads a list (as short as two, or as long as eight) of alternate letters and numbers. The person being tested must repeat them, putting the numbers first and in numerical order, followed by the letters in alphabetical order. For example, the psychologist reads, 'W-4-G-8-L-3', and the person being tested is expected to respond with, '3–4–8–G-L-W'. (Maximum of 30 trials)

Symbol Search. Identify, from a list of abstract symbols, which symbol in a given pair of target symbols is contained in the list. (As many as can be completed correctly in two minutes)

Coding. Write down the symbol that corresponds to a given number. An example of this type of task is shown in Figure 4. (As many as can be completed correctly in two minutes)

Cancellation. In a large sheet of paper with brown triangles and squares and blue triangles and squares, put a pencil line through each blue square and each brown triangle. There is a second sheet with red or yellow stars and circles. (The time to finish each sheet is taken)

That's the full WAIS-IV. Some of its fifteen tests involve language, some have numbers, some include shapes, and some are more abstract. Some are done at speed, within time limits, and some are not. Some involve memory and some don't. Some involve

1	2	3	4	5	6	7	8	9
>	—	≠	□	×	|	⌐	人	▽

Practice

4	8	9	1	2	6	3	5	7

Test

3	2	5	6	9	1	2	7	7

4	6	7	2	1	9	8	8	3

2	3	8	5	6	4	8	3	7

4. Part of a test that is quite like the coding test of the Wechsler Adult Intelligence Scale IV. The idea is to enter the symbol that corresponds to each number in the empty space provided. The score is the number of correct symbols entered in two minutes. In the real test there would be many more items available for completing.

reasoning with information given by the tester; some involve discovering rules; some involve articulating abstract principles; and some involve practical knowledge. Some involve knowledge picked up from education, and some don't. The tests tap quite a wide range of our mental functions: seeing similarities and differences, drawing inferences, working out and applying rules, remembering and manipulating mental material, working out how to construct shapes, processing simple information at speed, articulating the meaning of words, recalling general knowledge, explaining practical actions in everyday life, working with numbers, attending to details, and so forth. They are reasonably representative of the spread of contents scoured by IQ-type tests, that is, intelligence tests. Arguably, certain sorts of mental functions do seem to be poorly represented here, or not represented at all, but a wide range of thinking skills is tested. And, for those who wish to write these tests off as mere 'paper-and-pencil' tests, only three of the fifteen tests require the examinee to hold a pencil, and none requires the writing of words, letters, or numbers.

The WAIS-IV is developed and marketed by Pearson Education in the USA and the UK. This large company develops and markets a wide range of psychological tests around the world. When they were gathering validation information about the WAIS-IV in the USA, they tested 2,200 people aged from 16 to 90 years old during 2007 and 2008. Here, I discuss the data from the 1,800 people who were between 16 and 69 years old when they were tested, because they took all fifteen tests. As a group, when compared with the US Census, they were representative in sex, ethnicity, and geographical location. They had a good spread of educational backgrounds. They were healthy, their first language was English, and they were not psychologists. Each person was tested on the WAIS-IV's fifteen mental tests over a total time of an hour or two. The results of this big testing exercise repeat one of psychology's most surprising and most reproduced findings.

Before I describe that finding, consider the following question. What do you expect to see in the relations (correlations) between these fifteen different tests? A sensible guess, one that I shared before seeing data such as these, is that many of these mental functions have no relations with each other. That is, there might be no correlation between performance on some individual tests and on others. One might go further and guess that being good at some tasks might carry a price in being poor at others; this predicts a negative correlation between some tests. For example, people with better ability to see spatial patterns might have lower verbal ability. Or, perhaps those who can see small, pernickety details in pictures might be poorer when it comes to checking through lists at speed. Or, perhaps people with a good memory have a slower mental speed. A lot of intuitive opinion about mental capability runs along the lines of there being some cost for any mental benefit we possess.

None of those predictions is correct. There are 105 correlations when we look at all the pairings among the fifteen tests. Every correlation is positive; performing well on one of the tests tends to go with performing well on the others. There are no tests that are unrelated to any other one, that is, there are no near-to-zero correlations. There are no tests that are negatively related with other ones. Even the lowest correlation between any two tests is still a modest 0.21 (between Comprehension and Cancellation). The highest correlation—between Comprehension and Vocabulary—is 0.74. The average of the 105 correlations is 0.45. Thus, even the average correlation between these varied mental tests is sizeable. But, remember that we are talking about the tendencies within this large group of people, and that the correlations are not perfect; individuals will provide us with comforting exceptions to the overall trend.

The second important fact is that some sub-groups of the fifteen tests in the WAIS-IV collection associate more highly among themselves than with others. For example, the tests of Similarities, Vocabulary, Information, and Comprehension all have especially high associations with each other. The average of the six correlations among these four tests is 0.70. Thus, although they relate quite strongly to every test in the WAIS-IV collection, they form a pool of tests that are especially highly related among themselves. This is not surprising. These four tests all involve language, having learned facts, and understanding.

Within the WAIS-IV collection of tests there are four such pools of tests that have especially close associations among themselves, even though they still relate positively to all the others. For example, the same thing occurs with Digit Span, Arithmetic, and Letter–number sequencing. They form another pool, with an average correlation of 0.62. They relate positively with all of the other tests in the collection, but they relate especially highly with each other. These three tests involve numbers and the ability to hold lists in memory while manipulating them.

There are two other such pools of tests that correlate especially highly with each other. The four pools of tests are indicated in Figure 1, and are now described.

Note that an ellipse in Figure 1 with the label 'verbal comprehension' has arrows pointing to four tests: Similarities, Vocabulary, Information, and Comprehension. What this means is that there are such close associations among these tests that they can be collected together under a hypothetical entity called 'verbal comprehension'. This entity represents the finding that these four tests have closer associations among themselves than they do with other tests. There is no test called 'verbal comprehension'; it is the statistical overlap among these four individual tests, to which someone has applied a plausible-sounding name to capture the types of thinking required to do these four tests. It recognizes their especially close correlations. Do not think that there is something in the brain that does 'verbal comprehension'; again, this is a name applied to what seems to be common among the thinking required to do these tests.

We now consider the other pools of tests within the WAIS-IV that seem to hang together especially tightly. In Figure 1 the quite closely associated Block Design, Matrix Reasoning, Visual Puzzles, Figure Weights, and Picture Completion tests are collected under the heading 'perceptual reasoning'. The average of the ten correlations among these tests is 0.52. I think this publisher-given label captures the sorts of thinking that must be done to perform well on these tests, though it might as well have been called abstract reasoning.

The three tests that involve numbers and lists are collected under the heading 'working memory': Digit Span, Arithmetic, and

Letter-number Sequencing. Working memory is a label that psychologists use to describe the ability to hold information in memory and manipulate it at the same time. Imagine what has to be done in the digit span backwards test. A list of numbers is read out by the tester. The person being tested is asked to repeat it, but backwards. Therefore, at the same time as retaining the list, they have to reverse it in their mind and read out a reversed list. That hurts one's head—especially if the list is quite long—and the facility under strain is what psychologists call 'working memory'.

Finally, there are three tests that have a high association and all involve working at speed to make simple comparisons with, and simple decisions about, visual symbols: Symbol Search, Coding, and Cancellation. The average of the three correlations among these tests is 0.51. For these tests, each item is easy. If there were no time limit, very few people would make any mistakes. The key to performing well in these tests is correctly answering a large number of these easy items in a short time. They are collected under the label 'processing speed'. These tests contrast with the items in the other groups in which there are some hard items that one would not solve correctly no matter how long one had to think about them.

Here's a summary. A collection of fifteen varied mental tests given to 1,800 adult Americans found that people who are good at any one of the fifteen tests tend to be good at the other fourteen. In addition, there are sub-groups of tests that relate more highly to each other than to the tests in the other three pools. Figure 1 illustrates this latter fact by showing the related groups of tests collected together under headings or labels that summarize the sorts of mental skills common to the tests. Common names for these four collections of sub-groups are 'group factors of intelligence' or 'cognitive domains'. These domains of cognitive performance can be separated to a degree, because the tests within a domain relate to each other more strongly than they relate to tests in the other domains.

People can be given scores on the cognitive domains of 'verbal comprehension', 'perceptual reasoning', 'working memory', and 'processing speed'. Just as was done on the fifteen individual test scores, we can measure the correlations among the cognitive domains. That is, we can ask whether someone who is good at one of these domains of mental ability tends to be good at all the others. For example, do people with relatively good 'working memory' scores also have faster 'processing speed', better 'verbal comprehension' scores, and better 'perceptual reasoning' scores? The answer is yes: these four cognitive domains have correlations between 0.45 and 0.64. These are large associations. People who tend to score well in one of these domains tend to score well in all of the others. This is shown in Figure 1 by having all of the cognitive domains collected under a single heading of 'g', which, under a long-standing convention, denotes the 'general factor in intelligence'. Once again, it is a statistical distillation that describes a solid research finding: that is, that there is something shared by all the tests in terms of people's tendencies to do well, modestly, or poorly on all of them.

What comes next is important. The rectangles of the lower level in Figure 1 are actual mental tests—the fifteen individual tests—that make up the Wechsler Adult Intelligence Scale IV collection. The four ellipses that represent the cognitive domains (the middle level in the figure), and the ellipse that contains g (the top level in the figure) are optimal ways of representing the statistical associations among the tests contained in the rectangles. The things in the ellipses of the middle and top levels, the cognitive domains and 'g', do not equate to functions in the human mind; they are not bits of the brain. The names we pencil into the ellipses in the middle and top levels are common-sense guesses about what seems to be common to the sub-groups of tests that associate closely. The ellipses at those middle and top levels emerged from the statistical procedures and the data, not from intuition about the tests' similarities; however, the labels we write inside the ellipses are composed using common sense. It is important to appreciate that the analysis of mental tests that we deal with here just classifies the tests' statistical associations: it does not discover the systems into which the brain partitions its activities. However, it could hint at them, and that would need further research.

This way of describing people's differences in human mental capabilities, as illustrated in Figure 1, is called a hierarchy. The message from this large study is that just under half of the differences among a large group of adults may be attributed to mental ability that is required to perform all tests; we call that g or 'general intelligence', or 'general cognitive ability', or 'general mental ability'. Therefore, it does make sense to refer to a general type of mental ability; talking about a single, general intelligence has some veracity. There is something common to people's performance differences across many types of mental test.

It is important to be clear that g is a statistical result, but it is emphatically not a statistical artefact. That is, g need not appear. The analysis used to examine correlations among the tests does not force a g factor to emerge. If there were no tendency for the tests all to correlate positively in the manner that they do, there would be no g. I still find g to be a surprising result. We shall see, in the next part of this chapter, that g is a consistent finding when diverse cognitive tests are applied to a group of people.

It is also important to be clear that g does not explain all of the differences between people on those fifteen tests, only about 40 per cent or so. We can say with confidence that some people are generally cleverer than others, and also that there is more to human mental ability than just being generally clever. We see from Figure 1 that there are narrower types of ability than g—cognitive domains—and that these can be described in terms of the kinds of specific mental work needed to perform certain groups of tests. Last, the combination of general ability and cognitive domains is still not enough to account for differences

13

among people in how well they perform on the fifteen tests of the WAIS-IV. There is, in addition, some very specific ability needed to do well on each test. This is something that is not shared with any other test even where the material in the test is quite similar to that in some other tests.

When a person takes the fifteen tests of the Wechsler Adult Intelligence Scale IV, the psychologist can give them scores for each test, scores for each of the four domains, and a score for g. The g score is called 'Full Scale IQ' in the Wechsler test battery. Let's look at the distribution of that IQ score in the population. Have a look at Figure 5. Note that it is bell-shaped. This is also called a 'normal' curve. Along the bottom are IQ scores. The average (mean) IQ score is arbitrarily set at 100. Identify the IQ = 100 score along the bottom and note that the line that goes up from it hits the highest point in the curve. The height of the curve at any point is in proportion to the number of people in the population

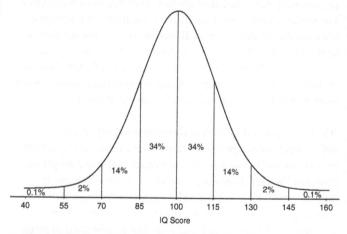

5. The distribution of IQ scores in the population. The mean is 100 and the standard deviation is 15. It shows the percentage of people with different IQ scores. Note that most people have scores around the mean, with fewer at the extremes.

14

who have that score. Therefore, scores become rarer as we move away from the average. Height has a similar-shaped curve, with most people being around the average; very tall and very short people are rarer. We have identified the mean IQ, at 100. This gives us the highest point of the curve. Next, we need a way of describing how the scores are distributed on either side of the mean. This aspect of the distribution of scores is called the standard deviation. In the Wechsler IQ scale the standard deviation is arbitrarily set at 15. In this shape of curve, this means that 34 per cent of people will be in the score range from the mean to one standard deviation above the mean, that is, 100 to 115; 14 per cent of people will have scores from 115 to 130, that is, between one and two standard deviations above the mean; 2 per cent of people will have scores from 130 to 145, that is, between two and three standard deviations above the mean. Only 0.1 per cent of people—one in a thousand—will have scores above 145, that is, more than three standard deviations above the mean. One can work out from the curve's shape that only one person in a million would have an IQ of 171 or higher. The same increasing rarity is found for scores below the mean. For example, only 2 per cent of people have IQ scores from 55 to 70. Only one person in a thousand has an IQ score below 55.

What the Wechsler Adult Intelligence Scale IV dataset tells us is that, in thinking about how well a person completes mental tests, we need to consider at least three questions. First, how strong is their general ability? Second, what are their strengths and weaknesses on the cognitive domains? Third, are there some individual tests on which they excel? There is also, in addition to these three levels of capability, luck and chance: some of the score that a person obtains on a test is down to whether or not they are having a good day. I hope that brings some order to the question of how many human cognitive abilities there are. The answer is that it depends on what level of specificity you have in mind. There is a general intelligence, and there are more specific mental capabilities.

The first person to discover the general factor in human intelligence was an English army officer turned psychologist, Charles Spearman, in a famous research paper in 1904. He examined schoolchildren's scores on different academic subjects. The scores were all positively correlated. He put this down to the children's having differences in a general mental ability. There followed decades of arguments among psychologists as to whether or not there was such a single entity. American psychologists, notably Louis Thurstone, suggested that there were about seven separable human mental abilities. He thought these were basic—he called them 'primary'—and he de-emphasized 'g'. However, the seven were positively correlated, even in his own dataset. The argument continued, and still does to an extent among people who don't know the research data. However, it was clear by the 1940s that, whenever a group of people was tested on a collection of mental tests, the correlations among the test scores were almost entirely positive. The general factor in mental ability was a substantial, inescapable fact. Just how inescapable this result is became clearer in the early 1990s.

Carroll's 'Human Cognitive Abilities' survey

In 1993, the American psychologist John Carroll brought out his book *Human Cognitive Abilities: A Survey of Factor Analytic Studies*. His career in academic psychology took him through most of the debates about the number and nature of human mental abilities. He saw that there was disagreement and that there were barriers to coming to a consensus. One problem was that there were hundreds of studies that had tested people on various mental ability tests. They tended to use different numbers and types of mental tests. The people tested in the studies were of different ages and backgrounds. The researchers used different statistical methods to help them decide on their conclusions about the numbers of mental abilities there were, and especially about whether there was a general intelligence factor. Carroll's purpose was to retrieve as many of the good-quality studies on human intelligence conducted during the 20th century as possible. He then re-analysed these studies using the same set of standard statistical methods. This involved his re-analysing over 400 sets of data, which included most of the large, well-known collections of data on human mental ability testing from the period. Therefore, if one knows what Carroll reported in his book, one knows most of the well-known data collected on human intelligence differences.

Carroll's book is over 800 pages long. The results are reported as statistical analyses and in technical jargon, but the conclusion was clear. In every dataset, he found the same pattern of correlations that we saw with the WAIS-IV. People who did well on one mental test tended to do well on the others. There were some sub-pools of tests with especially high associations. The datasets had a general cognitive ability factor accounting for a substantial amount of people's differences on the individual mental tests.

The essence of Carroll's findings appears on page 626, a diagram he called the 'three stratum model' of human cognitive ability. A simpler version of it is shown here as Figure 6. It has a structure very similar to the one in Figure 1. At the top of his hierarchy is his 'stratum III', or 'general intelligence' as he termed it. At 'stratum II' there are eight broad types of mental ability, four of which are similar to those cognitive domains we saw in the WAIS-IV. Carroll found more groups of mental capabilities, because he looked at data sets that included more, and more different, types of mental test than those in the WAIS-IV collection. At 'stratum I—shown here as sets of arrows—there were very specific mental skills, much like the ones specific to individual ability tests we saw in the WAIS-IV. Again, as we found with the WAIS-IV data, Carroll's strata of mental abilities emerged as the results from a standardized statistical procedure. Carroll did not impose a structure on the data. He discovered rather than invented the hierarchy of intelligence differences. General intelligence emerges, unforced, from every dataset in which several mental tests are taken by large numbers of people. Carroll's is the best-available

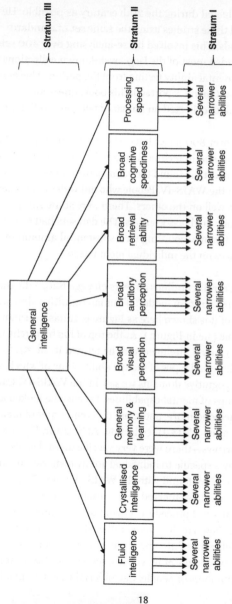

6. A hierarchical representation of the associations among mental ability test scores. The diagram represents the result of decades of work by John B. Carroll who re-analysed over 400 large, classic databases on human intelligence research.

survey of the hierarchy, but it had been appreciated long before his book in 1993. The British psychologists Cyril Burt and Philip E. Vernon had explicitly discussed intelligence differences in this hierarchical form in their respective books in 1940.

The bottom line is this. When people obtain a good score on a mental test, it is for at least four possible and non-exclusive reasons: they are good at mental tests overall (they have high general intelligence); they are good at that sort of test (they have a high ability for that cognitive domain); they are good at that specific test (they have high ability for that specific cognitive task); and they had the wind behind them on the day (chance favoured them on the testing occasion).

Charles Spearman's discovery of universally positive correlations among mental tests, his *g* factor, is a much-replicated empirical finding. I don't know a relevant dataset that failed to find it. Russell Warne extended this much-replicated phenomenon to thirty-one non-Western nations. In ninety-seven samples with more than 50,000 people tested on multiple cognitive tests, almost all of them showed a general cognitive factor. As found elsewhere, it accounted for about 46 per cent of the total test score differences among people. Therefore, we can nowadays describe the structure of mental test performances quite reliably. There is even a growing scientific effort to ask whether there is something like general intelligence in different non-human species of animals.

However, and emphatically, this is not proven to represent a model of the organization and compartments of the human brain. I do not think the empirical finding of *g* is a theory of intelligence differences. Rather, it is something that needs explaining. In the chapters that follow, we shall often see that the general factor of intelligence is the most influential aspect of intelligence test scores. For example, the ability of cognitive tests to predict educational, occupational, and health outcomes is mostly due to the general intelligence factor. The genetic influences are, too. And the effects of ageing are to a substantial extent on the g factor. The influences of ageing, though, are more subtle than that. We shall read, in Chapter 2, that age wears away at some cognitive domains and leaves others largely intact. With ageing, an important distinction emerges between those stratum II abilities that are part of so-called 'fluid' and 'crystallized' intelligence.

'Intelligence' beyond intelligence tests

The universal finding of the g factor and the hierarchy might surprise those who have heard of or read Howard Gardner's popular writings on 'multiple intelligences'. He suggested that there are many forms of mental ability and that they are unrelated. However, his ideas are limited by the lack of data that have been collected to test them. The facts are that some of Gardner's supposedly separate intelligences are well known to be correlated positively and linked thereby to general mental ability, such as his verbal, mathematical, and musical intelligences. Some of his so-called intelligences, though valued human attributes, are not normally considered to be mental abilities, that is, not within humans' cognitive sphere. For example, his physical intelligence is a set of motor skills and interpersonal intelligence involves personality traits.

Gardner had a point, though. Tests of mental abilities such as were described above do not assess all important aspects of humans' psychological differences. Standard cognitive tests do not measure creativity or wisdom, for example. Neither of these valued qualities is easy to measure—psychologists do not have a good grip on them—though both have some demonstrable associations with intelligence. Mental ability tests do not measure personality traits (e.g. neuroticism, extraversion, conscientiousness, and agreeableness), social adroitness, leadership, charisma, cool-headedness, altruism, or many other things that we might recognize as having individual differences.

That proper point is not the same as saying that intelligence-type tests are useless.

I should say one last thing here, before we continue to the nine other quite interesting things about intelligence. I am not invoking or inventing an entity of intelligence. I use that word as a shorthand for scores on cognitive (mental ability) tests. Therefore, what we look at in Chapters 2 to 10 are nine more quite interesting things about intelligence test scores.

Chapter 2
What happens to intelligence as we grow older?

Most people of middle and older age are willing to concede that their physical prowess in many areas is not as good as it was when they were in their twenties and thirties. They sometimes complain with a hint of humour that their memory is not what it was, or that they don't think as quickly as they used to. But people don't tend to say that they are becoming less intelligent as they grow older.

People who experience greater age-related declines in intelligence are at greater risk of dementia, and of dying earlier. And older people with greater cognitive decline tend to have lower quality of life, are less able to carry out their tasks of daily living, and are less able to live independent lives. Therefore, finding out if and why some people's thinking skills age better than others' is practically important. That is one of the main aims of my own research team, and it is the topic of this chapter.

Salthouse's Virginia studies

Here we will see Timothy Salthouse, one of the major international figures in cognitive ageing, asking whether being older affects the cognitive domains. This study falls between being a dataset and a meta-analysis, because Salthouse put together many of his own datasets to make sample sizes of between 2,369 and 4,149 people. The participants were from about 20 to over 85 years old. Each of them took some subset of sixteen different cognitive tests.

The list of cognitive tests was composed by Salthouse to represent different cognitive domains. There were memory tests, for example remembering lists of unrelated words, and remembering which words were paired with others in lists of word pairs. There were reasoning tests, for example a test like the matrices test we saw in Chapter 1, and a test in which one had to complete series (e.g. H-C-G-D-F-?). There were tests of spatial visualization, for example having to work out how a folded page with a hole punched through its layers would look when unfolded, and which of a series of three-dimensional structures corresponded to a two-dimensional pattern. There were tests of speed, for example a coding test similar to the one in Chapter 1, and a test where pairs of patterns were shown and the task was to write S if the two were the same and D if the two were different. There were vocabulary knowledge tests, for example having to define the meaning of words, and having to choose which of a list means the opposite of a given word. In all, there were three tests for each cognitive domain, except for vocabulary, which had four.

To be clear: each person was tested only once. This study was about how people of different ages scored on the cognitive tests. This is called a cross-sectional study. Have a look at Figure 7. Along the bottom is the age, from about 20 years to the 80s. Up the left-hand side is the score on the cognitive domain. What's used here is a type of standard score, where 1 would equal about 15 points on an IQ scale of the type we saw in Figure 5. The names of the cognitive domains are given in a list in Figure 7.

Look at the 'Memory' line in Figure 7; it is the one with white diamonds. At each age, the average score is shown; this can be obtained by looking at the marker for a given age, and looking horizontally to the left until the score is seen. The test score at

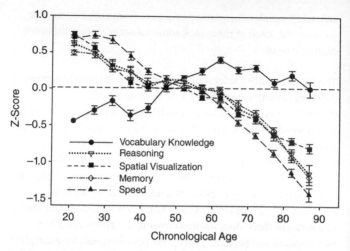

7. **Mean test scores of cognitive domains at different ages for participants taking part in cognitive ageing studies by Professor Timothy Salthouse.**

each age also has a standard error. These are the little T-shaped things coming out, up and down, from the circles, triangles, and squares; because they are small, they mean that measurement here was accurate. Memory scores are generally higher at the younger ages and lower on average at the older ages. It also appears that the age association is not a straight line downwards from the twenties to the eighties. The downward slope from the twenties to the late fifties or 60 is quite shallow, especially from about 35 to about 60. The slope from the late fifties or 60 to the eighties is steeper. On average, older people do less well on memory tests than younger people, but there might be a steeper decline in the average score after about 60 years of age. The results for Reasoning and Spatial Visualization show a similar pattern. They also have a general downward trend from young adulthood, and a steeper downward slope after about 60 years old. For these three types of test, note the overall size of the lowering in average score from the youngest to the oldest ages. It is quite

24

large, being about one and a half standard units. If this were an IQ scale, it would be about 20 or more points. If we were to accept that these results represent ageing-related changes, then we could conclude that average scores on memory, reasoning, and spatial visualization go down a bit from young adulthood to late middle age, with a steeper decline from then to old age.

The other two types of test—Processing speed and Vocabulary— look different in their age patterns.

Speed is marked by black triangles in Figure 7. The average scores go down in a fairly straight line from about 30 to the eighties. The difference between about age 30 and the eighties is about two standard units, which is about 30 points in an IQ scale. If we were to accept that these results represent ageing-related changes, we would conclude that average processing speed declines steadily and substantially from young adulthood to older age; older people think much more slowly on average than younger people.

If this seems discouraging, it is not all bad news. Vocabulary is marked with black circles in Figure 7. The overall pattern is that the average scores go up from young adulthood and peak around 60 years old. This is a cognitive domain that has its pinnacle in late middle age and early older age. Note, also, that scores in the eighties are still better than those in young adulthood.

Other large cross-sectional studies find the same as Salthouse— including the Wechsler tests—with the added good news that some number skills and knowledge also age relatively well. Longitudinal studies—in which the same people are tested repeatedly as they grow older—find similar results to those described above, after the effects of test familiarity and practice are taken into account.

If we were asked, 'what happens to intelligence on average as people grow older?,' we would have to equivocate and respond: 'It depends on which cognitive domains you are referring to.' Some, but not all, aspects of cognitive function show lower average scores in older people. This age-related finding—and the differential effects of some causes of neurological damage—are captured in an important division of intelligence into 'fluid' and 'crystallized'. This was suggested by Raymond Cattell and John Horn. Fluid intelligence tends to be assessed using unfamiliar materials, requiring active thinking, and often under time pressure. It declines on average with age. Crystallized intelligence tends to be assessed using tests of knowledge—such as vocabulary, general knowledge, or some number skills—and relies more on asking what a person knows than requiring them actively to work something out on the spot. Fluid and crystallized intelligence, though separable, are correlated; people high on one tend to be high on the other one.

Does intelligence 'all go when it goes'?

We have just seen how cognitive domains change with age. Let's now bring general intelligence into the picture. We know from Chapter 1 that cognitive domains are all highly correlated. So, we now ask this: if someone is experiencing age-related decline on one cognitive ability, do they tend to be declining on all others too? This is often posed in a vernacular way: 'does it all [i.e. all the different cognitive domains] go together when it goes?' Elliot Tucker-Drob conducted a meta-analysis on the topic, which he and his co-authors described as 'coupled cognitive changes'. He put it as follows: 'It is critical to know whether individual differences in longitudinal changes interrelate across different cognitive abilities.'

Tucker-Drob found twenty-two separate datasets, with a total of more than 30,000 participants. Each of these datasets had participants who had taken multiple cognitive tests at multiple times as they aged, from twice to twelve times. The average period of follow-up was about ten years. People in these studies started being tested at between 35 years of age and 85 years of age, with an average of 67 years. The cognitive tests taken included different types of memory, processing speed, spatial ability, reasoning, and verbal knowledge. The average decline was an equivalent of about 7½ points on an IQ score per ten years.

Tucker-Drob's result was that, 'on average, 60% of individual differences in ageing-related cognitive change is shared across abilities'. That means that 60 per cent of people's differences in ageing-related change in diverse cognitive tests and cognitive domains is due to change in general intelligence. He explains, 'This relatively high estimate indicates that individuals who decline precipitously in, for example, processing speed relative to their peers, are also likely to be declining in, for example, reasoning and episodic memory relative to their peers.' Yes, therefore, to a substantial extent, it (intelligence) does all tend to go when it goes.

Tucker-Drob made a clear warning. Just because quite a substantial proportion of people's cognitive changes (typically, we mean declines) across different cognitive domains can be captured by a single, general dimension, this does not imply that there is a single cause. He also suggested that this single dimension of cognitive decline could have large numbers of possibly independent social, biological, and genetic causes.

The Scottish Mental Surveys of 1932 and 1947

We have seen that, on average, scores on most cognitive domains and in general intelligence decline with older age. We now ask whether everyone follows that average. Do people differ in how much their intelligence changes from youth to older age? To answer this question, a cross-sectional study will not do. What we need is something unusual, that is, we need intelligence test scores on the same people across a long period of time. Scotland has provided this in the form of the Scottish Mental Surveys of 1932 and 1947 and their follow-up studies. Elsewhere in this book, we shall use these surveys to exemplify other aspects of intelligence research, so I am going to describe them now in some detail.

On Monday, 1 June 1932, almost every child attending school in Scotland who was born in 1921 sat the same intelligence test. It was a massive national study that has never been repeated in any other country in the world. Almost the entire population of 10½- to 11½-year-olds took the test under the same conditions. It was organized by the Scottish Council for Research in Education. The study was called the Scottish Mental Survey 1932. The Survey's data were collected to assist in educational provision and to measure the number of children with educational special needs in schools. Teachers did the testing and the scoring of the tests. The test was invented and provided by the then-famous educational psychologist Godfrey Thomson from the University of Edinburgh. He was the originator of the Moray House Tests that were used in the United Kingdom as '11-plus' intelligence tests for selection into different types of secondary schooling. The intelligence test used in the Scottish Mental Survey 1932 was a variation of the Moray House Test No. 12 (Figure 8). For forty-five minutes on a summer's day in 1932, 87,498 children applied their brainpower to answer questions about words, sentences, numbers, shapes, codes, instructions, and other miscellaneous mental tasks.

The Scottish Council for Research in Education did another whole-population survey of intelligence, on Wednesday, 4 June 1947. Almost every child in Scotland who was born in 1936 and who was at school sat the Moray House Test No. 12. This was the Scottish Mental Survey 1947. It tested 70,805 children.

Until about the 1960s the Scottish Mental Surveys were famous for their uniqueness in having tested almost entire year-of-birth populations. Several scholarly books were published with the statistical data from them. However, as the 11-year-olds from the

THE SCOTTISH COUNCIL FOR
RESEARCH IN EDUCATION

1932
MENTAL SURVEY
TEST

*SUITABLE FOR PUPILS OF
TEN AND ELEVEN YEARS OF AGE*

*MENTAL SURVEY TEST, 8 pp., 4d.
PRELIMINARY PRACTICE TEST, 2 pp., 1d.
INSTRUCTIONS FOR ADMINISTRATION,
8 pp., 4d.*

SPECIMEN SET - *9d., post free*

UNIVERSITY OF LONDON PRESS LTD.

WAR-TIME ADDRESS:
ST HUGH'S SCHOOL, BICKLEY, KENT

8. Cover of the Moray House Test used in the Scottish Mental Survey
1932.

1932 Survey reached middle and older age, the data gathered dust in a series of Edinburgh attics and basements. Psychologists interested in the study of human intelligence differences had all but forgotten about the results of the Scottish Mental Surveys of 1932 and 1947.

Through a sequence of accidents, I learned about the surveys and worked with Professor Lawrence Whalley, then at the University of Aberdeen, to find them. His wife Patricia tracked down the survey data to a safe, locked cage in the basement of the then offices of the Scottish Council for Research in Education in St John Street, Edinburgh. In a series of ledgers, the more-than-sixty-year-old data of the 1932 Survey were preserved, recorded in the neat handwriting of the 1930s teachers. The 1947 Survey's data were there too, in typed sheets bound in books. Each region of Scotland had its own ledgers. Each of the region's schools had its own pages in the ledger. And each line of each ledger contained a pupil's name, date of birth, and score from the Moray House Test No. 12 of general intelligence.

As Lawrence and I literally blew dust from these ledgers, we started to appreciate how valuable these data might be. In recent years, the Western world's populations had changed, with a higher proportion of older people. It emerged that one of the predictors of higher quality of life in older age is avoiding cognitive decline. But, to find out whether people have or have not retained their intellectual abilities, one needs to know what people's cognitive functions used to be like, when they were young and healthy. Though there were some studies that followed up people as they grew older, none had been able to relate intelligence in childhood to intelligence in older age. Therefore, no other studies had asked about people's different amounts of relative change over that long period. With the re-emergence of the data from the Scottish Mental Surveys of 1932 and 1947, we saw the possibility of studying each individual's change in intelligence over almost the whole human life course. However, to conduct such a study, we would have to find those same 1932- and 1947-born people in older age.

We did trace some surviving participants of the Scottish Mental Surveys. Our first aim was to discover how stable intelligence was from age 11 years to older age. Because they were already quite old in the late 1990s, our research began with the survivors of the earlier, 1932 Survey, that is, of those born in 1921. We tried to find some of the still-healthy people who took part in the Scottish Mental Survey 1932. Advertisements were placed in the media. Our researchers contacted people via their general medical practitioners. We began on a smaller scale in Aberdeen, setting up the Aberdeen Birth Cohorts of 1921 and 1936. We conducted larger studies in Edinburgh, forming the Lothian Birth Cohorts of 1921 and 1936. We hired Aberdeen's Music Hall for the morning of 1 June 1998 and set it out as an examination hall. We obtained a copy of the original Moray House Test No. 12 that was used in 1932, and we reprinted it. We made small changes to two questions to prevent anachronisms in the test. Exactly sixty-six years to the day after they first sat the test, seventy-three people came along to resit the test that they had last seen as young schoolchildren (Figure 9). I read aloud the instructions exactly as they had been by teachers in 1932. We applied the same forty-five-minute time limit. A meeting some weeks later increased our numbers to 101.

By the end of this exercise, we had scores on the same intelligence test for the same people at age 11 and at age 77 years. How similar would people's relative test scores be across that long period, covering most of the human life course? In addition to being interesting, the results are potentially useful. If there are people whose scores have aged well, they might have some lessons for us about successful ageing.

Figure 10 shows the results. It is a 'scattergram', that is, a diagram with a scatter of points; here, they are crosses. Each

9. Photograph of members of the Scottish Mental Survey 1932 who returned after 66 years to sit the same mental test that they had taken at age 11 on 1 June 1932. The venue was the Music Hall in Aberdeen. The date was 1 June 1998.

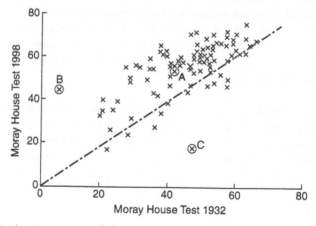

10. A scattergram graph that compares people's scores on the Moray House Test in 1932 (at age 11 years) and in 1998 (at age 77). Some crosses represent more than one person.

cross on the diagram represents at least one person from the 101 mentioned above. Each cross is a combination of the raw scores of the Moray House Test No. 12 taken by a single person at age 11 and at age 77. These are not IQ scores. They are scores out of 76, which is the best one can score on this test. How far the cross is along the horizontal shows the score that a given person obtained the first time they took the intelligence test at age 11. How far the cross is up the vertical shows the score that the person obtained the second time they took the intelligence test at age 77. The diagonal line in the diagram is the line along which all the crosses would rest if mental test scores were perfectly stable over time; that is, if every person got the same score the first and second time they tried the intelligence test, all the crosses would fall on that diagonal line.

The crosses don't all fall on that line. They deviate from the pattern of perfect stability in two ways. First, most of the crosses fall above the diagonal line. That means that most people scored better the second time they took the test: the group, on average, improved over time. People do a bit better on the Moray House Test No. 12, on average, at age 77 than they did at age 11. However, that's not the interesting part of the results.

Second, there is a general pattern of crosses going from the bottom left of the graph to the top right. There aren't many crosses in the top left or bottom right of the graph's area. But there is some spread, so that the correlation is not perfect. Some people did better than their first score and some did a bit worse, but there is still quite a strong tendency for the people who did relatively well first time round to do relatively well on the second test. This is an important finding: largely speaking, the people who did well in this intelligence test in 1932 also tended to do well in 1998. Those who did more poorly as children tended to stay near the bottom. Most people fall along a line which indicates general consistency in scores. The correlation between scores at age 11 and at age 77 was 0.63, which is large. As an added technicality, the people we got back to take the test in 1998 were not fully representative of the whole population. On average they were better intelligence test scorers than the full population, and they tended not to have such a wide spread in scores. This narrowing of the range of scores lowers our correlation from the true value; it seemed that 0.7 might be nearer to the true association than 0.6 over sixty-six years.

It is interesting to look at how some individuals changed from childhood to older age. There are crosses marked A, B, and C in Figure 10. Person A has an about-average score at age 11 and again at age 77. B and C are two people who show large changes between 1932 and 1998. Person B had about an average score in 1998, but a low score when tested in school sixty-six years earlier. Therefore, they improved their ranking a lot between childhood and older age. Person C had about an average score in 1932 but was equal-lowest when we tested people in 1998, representing a dramatic drop in relative performance. Sadly, we discovered later that Person C in Figure 10 was in the early stages of Alzheimer's dementia.

We have replicated the lifetime-long intelligence association since then, with our other follow-up studies of the Scottish Mental Surveys. The correlation was 0.66 in 485 people of the Lothian Birth Cohort 1921 who took the Moray House Test at age 11 and age 79. When the Lothian Birth Cohort 1921 reached 90 years old they took the Moray House Test No. 12 again; the correlation between the age 11 and age 90 intelligence test scores was 0.51. In 1017 participants of the Lothian Birth Cohort 1936 the correlation between Moray House Test score at age 11 and age 70 was 0.67. Overall, then, we have a robustly replicated and large association between intelligence in childhood and older age; it's not far from 0.7.

To explain what these results mean, consider this: a correlation of about 0.7 means that about 50 per cent of the differences in intelligence in older age are accounted for by the test scores at age 11. Technically, one gets the proportion of variance shared at the two ages by squaring the correlation. There is therefore a large amount of stability in people's rank order of intelligence test scores between childhood and older age. However, there's then the other 50 per cent to consider. This means that about half of the differences in people's intelligence test scores in older age are not accounted for by their childhood intelligence. People shift up and down a bit in their rank order of intelligence from childhood to older age. A main aim of my research team is to find likely sources of that half of intelligence variation in older age that was not there in youth. Part of that will be error of measurement; one cannot measure intelligence perfectly either in childhood or in older age. However, the fact that 50 per cent of people's differences in intelligence in older age were not there in youth means that we should seek the causes of that part of people's differences in intelligence in older age that is not accounted for by childhood intelligence. Are there lifestyle, medical, genetic, or other factors that help some people's brains negotiate the adult life course better than others? Look again at Figure 10 and look at scores of, say, 40 along the bottom. Now, move vertically from there. Children with scores of about 40 have a range of scores in older age. A key job for today's researchers is to find out why some of those with any given score in childhood have done better or worse than others in older age.

The answer to the question, 'do people differ in how much their intelligence changes from youth to older age?' is yes. Next, we want to know why.

Preventing some age-related cognitive decline

We now enquire why some people's intelligence ages better than others'. It is best not to offer any single dataset here. Many factors might be risks for steeper, age-related cognitive decline. Others might help prevent some of it. No one study can cover enough of them. Also, most studies are observational: they correlate a potential risk or protective factor with cognitive function in older age, or cognitive change in older age. However, such observations often don't translate into causal information. A stronger type of study is the randomized controlled trial, in which people are randomly allocated to one treatment or another, or none. For example, if the idea was that physical exercise might help people's cognitive functions to decline less steeply with age, then some people might be allocated to an exercise regimen, and some not. There are not many of these types of study, and they can't be done for every possible intervention. For example, if the idea was that smoking was harmful to cognitive ageing, one would not set up a trial in which some people were allocated to be smokers.

There's another problem with observational studies. It is called confounding. To illustrate this, we shall take an example from the Lothian Birth Cohort 1936, reported by my colleague Janie Corley. In one study, when they were 70 years old, we asked the participants how much alcohol they drank, and what types of alcohol. They were modest drinkers, not heavy. We calculated the average number of standard units of alcohol they drank each day. We found that those who drank more alcohol tended to have better scores on general intelligence, processing speed, and memory. The associations were small, but they were statistically significant and consistent, occurring in both men and women. When I present this to scientific and lay audiences, they tend to cheer. But they have celebrated too early. They forget that the Lothian Birth Cohort 1936 has scores on an intelligence test from the age of 11 years. What happens if one adjusts these alcohol-drinking versus cognitive-function-at-age-70 associations for the IQ scores obtained at age 11? That is, what happens if we ask, effectively, the question: does alcohol drinking have an association with change in intelligence from childhood to age 70? The answer is that the results largely disappear. It seems that the reason for the slight association between drinking more alcohol and higher intelligence at age 70 is not that alcohol is keeping people mentally sharp. No, it appears, instead, that children who are more intelligent also tend to be more intelligent at age 70, and tend to drink a bit more alcohol (modestly). This is confounding, that is, the contemporaneous association between alcohol drinking and intelligence at age 70 is confounded by intelligence test scores at age 11. For men, the non-drinkers at age 70 had a mean childhood IQ of 96, the low-level drinkers' IQ at age 11 was 98, and the moderate drinkers' IQ at age 11 was 104. There was a small positive correlation (0.19) between intelligence test score from age 11 and amount of alcohol drinking at age 70. The correlation was strongest between intelligence at age 11 and the amount of red wine drunk at age 70 (0.25). Another result was that people whose jobs had been more professional tended to drink more alcohol overall (correlation = 0.16), and more red wine within that (correlation = 0.29). The association between more alcohol drinking and intelligence at age 70 might, therefore, have a life-history/lifestyle explanation. That is, brighter children might tend to have more education, and in turn tend to progress to more professional jobs, and part of all that is probably a lifestyle tendency that includes regular modest drinking of alcohol, especially red wine (and maybe gin and tonic, I speculate).

Let's now go back to asking: 'why does some people's intelligence age better than others?' Brenda Plassman did a systematic review on this topic. Her team searched for observational and intervention studies that had sought evidence for factors that were risks for accelerated cognitive decline, or were protective against it. It was not a meta-analysis: the studies were not sufficiently similar to allow their results to be analysed together. She found 127 observational studies, 22 randomized controlled trials, and 16 previous systematic reviews. The cognitive outcomes used in the studies ranged from the general intelligence factor we saw in Chapter 1 (composed from several diverse tests) to single and rather crude estimates of cognitive function. The results are not easy to summarize. That's not the fault of Plassman and team, it is because the research is scrappy.

From observational studies, Plassman found evidence that those people (about a quarter of the population) who have a certain version (the e4 allele) of the gene for Apolipoprotein E on chromosome 19 tend to have slightly steeper cognitive decline in older age. This genetic variant is a risk factor for dementia, and it appears to be a risk factor for slightly steeper cognitive ageing also in those without dementia. She also found that possible risk factors for steeper cognitive ageing included smoking, depression, and diabetes. Factors for which there is some evidence as protective against steeper cognitive decline included eating the Mediterranean diet, eating more vegetables, being in more professional occupations, and taking part in some leisure activities.

For factors that had been the subject of both observational studies and randomized controlled trials, there was some evidence that greater physical activity and cognitive engagement might be somewhat protective against steeper cognitive decline.

The study of cognitive ageing is one of the most lively and exciting in the field of human intelligence. It is also one of the most important, as the proportion of older people in the population grows larger and as people live longer.

Chapter 3
Are there sex differences in intelligence?

I struggle to give a good scientific reason for asking this question. I know that it interests many people. I know that it is controversial. My starting point for looking at any study of sex differences in intelligence would be: are there equally population-representative groups of males and females? It seems likely to me that almost any study of male versus female average intelligence will be scuppered by one sex's being more selected than the other. For example, women might be more likely to take part in studies. Equally representing males and females in a study might seem to be almost impossible. Unless, that is, there was a study that had recruited the whole population.

The Scottish Mental Survey 1932

I described the Scottish Mental Survey 1932 in Chapter 2. Recall that they were all born in 1921, and that the survey tested almost the whole Scottish population born in that year. We used all of its data in a report on female–male differences in intelligence.

First, consider the intelligence tests. The main intelligence test used was the Moray House Test No. 12. There were two other tests. These others were non-verbal tests. They did not use words, and so could be completed by children who could barely read or write. In the 'First Picture Test' there was a key that related simple line drawings of five everyday objects to the numbers 1 to 5. Using this key, the children were asked to write the correct number below 40 of these objects on a page. They were asked to complete as many as they could in one minute. Most children scored perfectly. The 'Second Picture Test' contained two practice items and seven test items. Each item had three line drawings on the left, and five items on the right, all in a row. One practice item had snowdrops, daffodils, and crocuses on the left. On the right were a bottle, a cup, a rose, a brush, and scissors. The child was asked to pick the item among the five on the right, 'that is most like the first three'. The child was given two minutes to complete the seven test items. This was meant to be an easy test, and most children scored perfectly. We summed children's scores on the three tests, that is, The Moray House Test No. 12, the First Picture Test, and the Second Picture Test. We converted the scores to an IQ scale with a mean of 100 and a standard deviation of 15.

Second, because getting as close as possible to the whole population of those born in 1921 was important, we should ask how closely we got to that. There were 87,498 children who sat the Scottish Mental Survey 1932's tests. The ledgers from Fife, Wigtown, and Angus are missing. That won't bias the sex-representativeness of the remainder. The available dataset had 86,520 children. There were 79,376 children (39,343 girls, and 40,033 boys) with scores on all three intelligence tests, and who did not score zero on either of the Picture Tests. Recall that the Scottish Mental Survey 1932 tested around 95 per cent of the 1921-born population still living at age 11. The data used in this study is approximately 91 per cent of that 95 per cent, that is, we studied about 86 per cent of a whole year-of-birth population.

This was as near to a whole population as was ever tested on an intelligence-type test. With almost 40,000 boys and girls in the sample, it had great sensitivity (power, for the statistically inclined) to detect even a very small sex difference in average intelligence. Almost all children are in primary education at age 11 in Scotland. There is no subject specialization at this age.

I now advise a quick look at Figure 5, for a refresher on the mean and the standard deviation. When we compare the girls and boys, we can ask if the means are the same, that is, if one group has a higher average intelligence test score than the other. We can also ask if the standard deviations are the same. Looking at Figure 5, that would be asking if one group's bell curve distribution is thinner or wider than the other's. A thinner curve would indicate more scores near the mean and fewer at the extremes. A wider bell curve would indicate fewer scores at the mean and more at the extremes.

Even with these large numbers of boys and girls, we found no significant difference in their mean intelligence score. The mean IQ score was 100.64 for girls and 100.48 for boys. Females and males are equally intelligent in that almost-whole population.

Then came a twist. We noticed that the boys' and girls' scores were not equally spread. The means were the same. However, the standard deviation for the boys was 14.9, and for the girls it was only 14.1. This difference in spread was statistically significant. Girls' scores were more clustered around the average scores. There were proportionately more boys at the extremes. Let us examine this sex difference in IQ-score spread more closely.

Figure 11 illustrates the boys' and girls' spreads in intelligence test scores. To show this, I clumped the boys and girls into IQ-based groups. The IQ groups are named along the bottom of the figure. At the low extreme, there was a group between IQ score 50 and just under 60. At the top extreme, there was a group from IQ score 130 to just under 140. In between, each group was 5 IQ points wide, that is, IQ score 60 to just under 65, 65 to just under 70, and so on all the way up to 125 to just under 130. As we would expect from the well-known bell-shaped distribution of

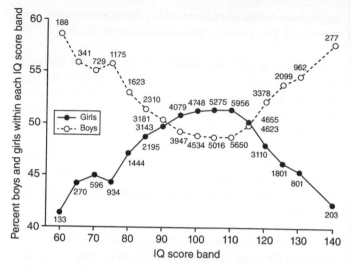

11. Numbers (beside each circle) and percentages (up the left-hand side) of girls and boys found within each IQ score band. This is almost all of the Scottish population born in 1921 and attending schools on 1 June 1932. They took part in the Scottish Mental Survey 1932. Note the slight excess of girls in the average scores, and the slight excess of boys at the lower and higher scores.

intelligence, there are much larger numbers of people with scores around the average than there are at the high and low extremes. Those are the numbers beside the circles. Then we asked how many boys and girls there were in each IQ group. In Figure 11, look at the middle-scoring groups, from 90 to 110. Note that there are large numbers of girls and boys beside each black and white circle. Here, boys make up less than half of the population at that level of intelligence (48.7 per cent), and there is an excess of girls. The difference—the gender gap—is a few per cent. Now, move to the extremes. Note the smaller numbers of boys and girls beside the white and black circles. That's what we expect in extreme scores, following the bell-curve distribution. In the lowest group, up to a score of just under 60, there are 58.6 per cent boys, and the gender gap is 17.2 per cent. In the highest group, where the scores go from 130 to just under 140, there are 57.7 per cent boys, and the gender gap is 15.4 per cent.

In this large dataset, on almost a whole population, there is no difference in the average intelligence of males and females at age 11 years. However, there are sex differences in the spread of the IQ scores. More girls have scores around the mean. The boys' IQ score distribution is more extreme, with greater proportions at the lower and higher levels of intelligence.

No one dataset is likely to settle an issue. Here we can ask the following questions. These were data from a long time ago: is the result found in more recent studies? These were data from 11-year-olds: is the result found after adolescence? These were data from a test of general intelligence: is the result found for specific types of intelligence? We shall now answer these questions.

The National Longitudinal Survey of Youth 1979

We used this sample to look at male–female differences in general intelligence in more recent times, and in mostly post-adolescent young adults. Therefore, it addresses two questions that I asked at the end of the section on the Scottish Mental Survey 1932-based study. The National Longitudinal Survey of Youth 1979 is based in the United States, and it makes its data available to researchers around the world.

The people who took part in this study were aged between 14 and 22 years old on 1 January 1979. There were 12,686 people in the sample. It was designed to be a close representation of non-institutionalized young people in the USA. We did not rely on the samples of young men and women being representative of the USA's population. We found out that this sample had many siblings. We thought it would be a good idea to select opposite-sex siblings to examine sex differences in intelligence. That would be a neat way of controlling for many issues that might otherwise bias the samples of males and females. For example, selecting opposite-sex siblings matches them on family background and to some extent for genetic factors. Looking at the National Longitudinal Survey of Youth 1979's dataset, we found 1,292 sibling pairs. They were close in their mean age, with females at 18.4 years (standard deviation 2.1) and males at 18.4 years (standard deviation 2.1).

As a part of the study, the participants took an intelligence test called the Armed Services Vocational Aptitude Battery. This has ten subtests: science, arithmetic, word knowledge, paragraph comprehension, numerical operations, coding speed, auto and shop information, mathematics knowledge, mechanical comprehension, and electronics information. We estimated, for each person, a general intelligence score based on all ten subtests. We noted that several tests are of a practical nature. Therefore, we checked the results by making a general intelligence score from only the four less vocationally oriented tests, that is, arithmetic, word knowledge, paragraph comprehension, and mathematics knowledge. This shorter composite is called the Armed Forces Qualification Test. Women scored better on some subtests, and men scored better on others. Our main aim, though, was to examine the brother–sister differences in general intelligence.

There were significant but very small advantages in the mean scores for males in the general intelligence estimate from both the broader Armed Services Vocational Aptitude Battery, and the narrower Armed Forces Qualification Test. The difference was less than a fifteenth of a standard deviation, that is, less than one IQ point. I think that is negligible.

A more striking difference was the spread of scores. The males' scores were more spread out than those of the females. The ratio of the male to female standard deviations was 1.16 for the Armed Services Vocational Aptitude Battery, and 1.11 for the Armed

Forces Qualification Test. In agreement with the results from the 11-year-olds of the Scottish Mental Survey 1932, these more recently born North American young adults showed the same pattern: males had more people at the lower and higher extremes of intelligence test scores than females, though the means were similar. We looked at the top 50 scorers on the Armed Forces Qualification Test, which is about the top 2 per cent in this sample: 33 were male and 17 were female.

The Cognitive Abilities Test 3 sample

Now, we move back to the United Kingdom. We examined another more up-to-date sample. This one could tell us about different domains of intelligence as well as general intelligence.

This dataset comes from school-based testing in the United Kingdom between September 2001 and August 2003. It is a massive dataset that is representative of United Kingdom schoolchildren aged 11 to 12 years. During that time, over half a million children sat the Cognitive Abilities Test 3 (CAT3). Most of the children sat the Level D version of the test, which is for 11- to 12-year-olds in the first year of secondary school. The mean age of the boys and girls was 11 years 7 months (standard deviation 4.4 months). The sample size was 324,000 children from 1,305 schools. This is about half of all the children of the United Kingdom in that age range. The CAT3 sample was very similar to all United Kingdom schools in terms of the proportions of boys and girls, whether the schools were selected for entry based on tests, the proportion of children entitled to free school meals, or proportions of children in minority ethnic groups and who had English as an additional language.

The CAT3 cognitive test battery has nine tests. There are three tests in each of three cognitive domains: verbal reasoning, quantitative reasoning, and non-verbal reasoning. The mean score over the three domains gives a general intelligence score. Because we focus here on the male–female differences in cognitive domains as well as on general intelligence, it is important to understand what cognitive tests are found in each domain. Here are example items, as described in the article by Steve Strand.

The verbal reasoning battery has tests of:

verbal classification, for example, 'Given three words belonging to one class, select which further word from a list of five belongs to the same class (e.g. eye, ear, mouth: nose, smell, head, boy, speak)';

sentence completion, for example, 'Selecting one word from a list of five (e.g. John likes to ___ a football match: eat, help, watch, read, talk)';

and verbal analogies, for example, 'Given one pair of words, complete a second pair from five possibilities (e.g. big → large; little → ?: boy, small, late, lively, more)'.

The quantitative reasoning battery has tests of:

number analogies, for example, 'Determine the relationship between the numbers in two example pairs and decide which of five options would complete a third pair in the same way (e.g. [9 → 3] [12 → 4] [27 → ?]: 5, 9, 13, 19, 21)';

number series, for example, 'Select one from five possible choices to complete the series (e.g. 2, 4, 6, 8, → ?: 9, 10, 11, 12, 13)';

and equation building, for example, 'Select the one answer choice that can be calculated by combining all the given elements to create a valid equation (e.g. 2 2 3 + ×: 6, 8, 9, 10, 11). Each element may be used only once, and there is only one correct answer.

The non-verbal reasoning battery has tests of:

figure classification, for example, 'Given three shapes belonging to one class, select which further shape from five alternatives belongs to the same class';

figure analogies, for example, 'Given one pair of shapes, complete a
    second pair from five possibilities';

and figure analysis, for example, 'A piece of paper is folded and holes
    are punched through the paper. How will the paper look when it
    is unfolded?'

First, let's consider the differences in mean scores between boys
and girls. Because the sample size is so massive—about a third of a
million children—almost any tiny difference will be statistically
significant. Indeed, the boy–girl differences were significant for all
three cognitive domains and for the general CAT3 score. Girls did
better than boys by 0.15 of a standard deviation in verbal ability,
which is equivalent to just over 2 IQ points. Boys did better than
girls on quantitative reasoning by 0.03 of a standard deviation,
which would translate to less than half an IQ point. Girls did
better than boys on non-verbal reasoning by about the same
amount. The overall mean CAT3 score of girls was 0.05 of a
standard deviation higher than boys, which is about three-quarters
of an IQ point. So, overall, there are some small differences in
scores that mostly favour girls.

We looked at the spread of scores. The standard deviations of the
boys were greater for all three domains, and for the overall CAT3
score (i.e. general intelligence). For verbal reasoning, the girls'
standard deviation was 14.5, and the boys' was 15.1. For
quantitative reasoning, the numbers were 13.8 versus 15.0, and for
non-verbal reasoning 13.9 versus 14.8. For the overall CAT3
score—general intelligence—the standard deviation for boys was
13.5 versus 12.7 for girls. In Figure 12 we used the same type of
diagram that we had used in Figure 11. Here, the CAT scores were
divided into nine groups, called stanines (standard nine scores).
There are much greater numbers, overall, in the middle groups
than at the edges. Look first at the bottom right, that is, at the
overall CAT3 score. As we found with the Scottish Mental Survey
1932 dataset, this much more recent large sample of children at

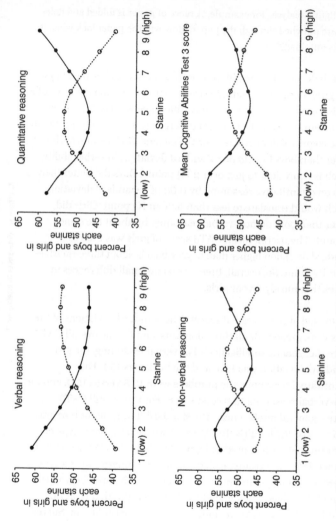

12. **The percentage of boys (closed circles) and girls (open circles) found in each standard nine ('stanine') score band from the Cognitive Abilities Test 3. The bottom-right graph is the average of the other three scores and is general mental ability (*g*).**

about the same age shows a similar pattern. That is, there is a greater proportion of girls than boys around the middle, which has the average scores. There are greater proportions of boys at the extreme scores. It does not look symmetrical, though; there are more boys than girls in the two top stanines and in the bottom three stanines. Non-verbal reasoning shows a similar picture. On quantitative reasoning, there are more boys than girls in the top three stanines, and in the bottom two. Verbal reasoning has a different pattern; there are more girls in the top five stanines and fewer in the lower stanines. For verbal reasoning, therefore, girls do better overall, and there is no tendency here for there to be more boys at the extreme high scores.

What we have found from these three studies is that there is little evidence of any average difference in intelligence between boys and girls, or young adults. Focusing just on the mean, though, hides an interesting difference. For overall, general intelligence, there are slightly more girls than boys in these samples around the average scores, and proportionately more males than females at the higher and lower extremes. This is found from decades-old and more recent studies, and in different tests, and in the USA as well as the UK. Among the cognitive domains, a different pattern occurred for verbal reasoning: there were more girls at the higher scores.

As a concluding comment, it should not be assumed that the small differences we have seen here in the standard deviations of intelligence test scores are enough to explain male or female overrepresentation in certain professions. That would have to be specifically investigated and shown. Also, we shall see in Chapter 7 that females have some ingredient(s) that turn the same level of intelligence into better academic qualifications.

Chapter 4
What are the contributions of environments and genes to intelligence differences?

We are now at the start of three chapters in which we ask about the origins of people's differences in intelligence. In Chapters 5 and 6, we will ask if clever people's brains run a bit faster, and if the structures of their brains have signatures of intelligence. First, though, let's ask whether genetic inheritance and the environments people experience affect intelligence differences. Researchers use two main resources to answer this question: twins and samples of deoxyribonucleic acid (DNA).

Twins

There are two types of twins: identical (monozygotic) and non-identical (dizygotic). Monozygotic twins develop from the same fertilized egg; therefore, they have the same genetic make-up. They are the same sex. Dizygotic twins develop from two different eggs that were fertilized by two different sperm; therefore, like siblings, they share half of their genetic make-up, and they might be the same or different in sex. That provides a natural experiment: there are two people of the same age, and in some cases they have the same genetic make-up and in some cases they share half of their genetic make-up.

What researchers want to know from twin studies is the extent to which people's differences on a trait are caused by their differences in genes and environments. A trait can be just about anything about a person that one can measure: for example, blood glucose level, height, weight, baldness, extraversion, or intelligence. The effect of the genes is usually called 'a', which is short for the additive effect of the genes. In twin research, it is usual to divide the environment into two aspects: shared and non-shared. Shared environment is sometimes called 'common' environment and shortened to 'c'. Non-shared environment is shortened to 'e'. Shared environment is those aspects of the environment that twins share. The most obvious aspects are the family, for instance having the same parents and being brought up in the same home. They might also share schools, and some teachers. Non-shared environment is those aspects of the environment that twins do not share. For example, they might suffer from different illnesses, they might have some different friends, and they might take different educational routes.

The assumption of researchers who use the twin method is that genes, shared environment, and non-shared environment might all contribute to people's differences in traits. They use samples of twins to estimate the proportions of these contributions. They do this by using some quite advanced statistical techniques, but we can understand the gist of it without being a statistician. A key to this is the between-twin correlation.

Usually, a correlation is between two things measured on the same people. I explain correlation at the end of this book. There, I write about a sample of people who had been measured on height and weight. Each person had a number for height and a number for weight. These were correlated to see if those who were taller tended to be heavier. This is usually set up as two columns of numbers in a table, with each person being a row in the table. The between-twin correlation is like this, with a twist. The twist is that we would test whether, when one member of a twin pair has a high score on a trait, the other member of the twin pair also scores highly. Assume we are measuring height. We would take the first member of each twin pair and create a column of numbers with their heights. Then we would take the second member of each of the twin pairs and list their heights on the next column, alongside their co-twin. In this case, we would have members of each twin pair as the rows. There's a further twist: we would do this separately for monozygotic and dizygotic twins. What this gives us is a correlation for a given trait between members of monozygotic twin pairs, and another correlation between members of dizygotic twin pairs. These correlations will tell us how similar identical and non-identical twins tend to be on the trait in question.

Before we ask how these two between-twin correlations can tell us about the contributions of genes (a), shared environment (c), and non-shared environment (e) to trait differences, it is useful to recap. First, monozygotic twins have the same set of genetic material, and dizygotic twins share just 50 per cent of their genetic material. Second, it is assumed that shared environment is just as similar in monozygotic and dizygotic twins. Third, non-shared environment is, by definition, completely different in the members of both monozygotic and dizygotic twin pairs. We can therefore describe the similarity between members of pairs of twins in simple equations. For monozygotic twins, the correlation between the pairs is composed of identical genes, and identical shared environments, and this degree of similarity is denoted as $1a + 1c$. For dizygotic twins, the correlation between the pairs is composed of 50 per cent shared genes and identical shared environments, and this similarity is denoted as $\frac{1}{2}a + 1c$. The shared environment (c) is thus assumed to make the same contribution in both types of twin. However, note that it is assumed that the genetic similarity has twice as much effect in monozygotic twins, and that that is the only difference between these types of twin pair. Therefore, a simple estimate of the genetic contribution to people's differences in a trait can be obtained by doubling the difference between the monozygotic and dizygotic correlation; this number would give the proportion of the given trait's differences that is due to genetic effects. Next, because the monozygotic correlation has all the genetic and the shared environment effects, we can estimate the size (proportion) of the non-shared environment effect by taking the monozygotic correlation away from 1. Last, we can estimate the size (proportion) of the shared environment effect by taking the genetic effect from the monozygotic correlation.

Here's a worked example. Let's say we measure a trait and we get a monozygotic correlation of 0.6, and a dizygotic correlation of 0.4. The genetic effect (a) is 0.4, that is, twice the difference between those correlations. That tells us that 40 per cent of people's differences in this trait are caused by genetic differences. Next, the non-shared environment effect (e) is 0.4, that is, 1 minus the monozygotic correlation. That tells us that 40 per cent of people's differences in this trait are caused by differences in non-shared environments. Last, the shared environment effect (c) is 0.2, that is, the monozygotic correlation minus the genetic effect. That tells us that 20 per cent of people's differences in this trait are caused by differences in the shared environments.

Although these computations using the monozygotic and dizygotic twins' correlations will not give bad answers, nowadays more sophisticated statistical modelling procedures are used. These procedures will estimate the a (genetic), c (shared environment), and e (non-shared environment) contributions, give the errors of their estimation, test whether they are significantly greater than zero, and provide a guide to how well the models fit the data. Nevertheless, research papers still tend to print the monozygotic and dizygotic correlations, and so the reader can usually make the simple calculations described above.

10,000+ twins, from three continents

I address the genetic and environmental contributions to intelligence differences using Claire Haworth's report. Her dataset has twins from several twin studies. There were 4,809 monozygotic twin pairs and 5,880 dizygotic twin pairs, overall.

The twin studies came from: Ohio USA (mean age 5 years), United Kingdom (mean age 12 years), Minnesota USA (mean age 13 years), Colorado USA (mean age 13 years), Australia (mean age 16 years), and the Netherlands (mean age 18 years). I will not describe all of the samples, but I will give some details of the largest one, from the United Kingdom.

The United Kingdom sample that contributed to this dataset was the Twins Early Development Study. There were 1,518 pairs of monozygotic twins, and 2,500 pairs of dizygotic twins. Of the latter, 1,293 were same-sex pairs, and 1,207 were opposite in sex. Each of the participants took four web-based cognitive tests. Three were from the Wechsler Intelligence Scale for Children. The other one was Raven's Matrices. From those four tests, a general intelligence score was calculated for each person. The social background of this sample is similar to the general UK population. Determining whether each pair of twins was monozygotic or dizygotic was tested using a questionnaire about physical similarity that was filled in by the parents. If there was any doubt, DNA was examined. The different twin samples in the report used different tests to assess intelligence.

For fun and instruction, we can perform a calculation of genetic and environmental contributions to intelligence test scores that was not done by Haworth and her co-authors. We can do this from the monozygotic and dizygotic twins' correlations reported in the paper. For the combined samples, the monozygotic twins' correlation for intelligence test scores was 0.76, and the dizygotic twins' correlation was 0.49. Using our formulae from above we can therefore estimate that: 54 per cent of the differences in intelligence are caused by genetic differences (that is, twice the difference between the monozygotic and dizygotic correlations is 0.54); 22 per cent of the differences are caused by shared environment (the monozygotic correlation of 0.76 minus the genetic effect of 0.54); and 24 per cent of the differences are caused by non-shared environment (1 minus the monozygotic correlation of 0.76). Roughly speaking, for this childhood-to-young-adulthood combined sample, about half of their differences in intelligence are caused by genetic differences and about half by environmental differences.

The details of Haworth's results are more interesting than that. The combined sample hides some changes in genetic and environmental contributions that happen from childhood to young adulthood. What she did next was to take the combined sample and separate the participants by age into children (mean age 9 years, range 4 to 10), adolescents (mean age 12, range 11–13), and young adults (mean age 17, range 14–34). The correlation for the monozygotic twins was 0.74 in childhood, 0.73 in adolescence, and 0.82 in young adulthood. The dizygotic correlation was 0.53 in childhood, 0.46 in adolescence, and 0.48 in young adulthood. Therefore, there is some tendency for monozygotic twins to become more similar in intelligence as they move from childhood to adulthood, and a slight move in the opposite direction for dizygotic twins. The authors themselves did a rough calculation—which you can do also—of the genetic contribution to intelligence at these different ages by doubling the difference between the monozygotic twins' and dizygotic twins' correlations. This gives the result that 42 per cent of children's intelligence differences are caused by genetic factors, rising to 54 per cent in adolescence, and rising further to 68 per cent in young adulthood. This is sometimes thought to be a counter-intuitive finding. However, before we consider it, we should examine the results of Haworth's formal statistical modelling.

Her modelling takes all the monozygotic and dizygotic twins' data and tries to find the genetic, shared environment, and non-shared environment values that fit best. It also provides standard errors for these estimates, so one can see how robust they might be. In fact, though the statistical modelling procedures can be abstruse, they are ultimately based on things like correlations, and we should not expect the results to be much different from the values estimated using the simpler method discussed earlier.

Haworth's modelling results are shown in Figure 13. Identify the axes first. Along the bottom, we see the three age groups: childhood, adolescence, and young adulthood. Up the left-hand side we see the percentage contribution to intelligence differences. There are three lines: one for genetics (A), one for shared environment (C), and one for non-shared environment (E). The vertical bars on each line are standard errors. The smaller these vertical bars are, the more confident one can be that the result is robust. These are OK-looking; they are not tiny, but they are not very big either.

The 'A' line in Figure 13 is the genetic contribution. The line goes up from left to right. That is, the genetic contribution to people's differences in intelligence is larger in adulthood than in

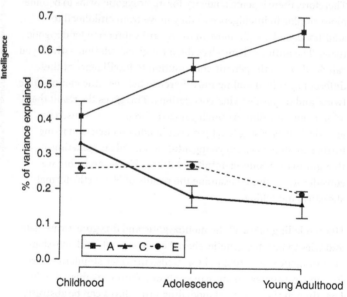

13. The different contributions (percentages up the left-hand side) of differences in genes (squares), shared environment (triangles), and non-shared environment (circles) to general cognitive ability at different ages (along the bottom).

childhood, with adolescence in the middle. We should be clear how one should state this. What this does not mean is, 'how much of my intelligence is caused by genetics'. No, what it estimates is the percentage of people's differences in intelligence that are caused by their genetic differences. In children, here, the answer is 41 per cent; in adolescents it is 55 per cent; and in young adults it is 66 per cent. So, by adulthood, two-thirds of people's differences in intelligence are caused by their genetic differences. The answer for childhood is about two-fifths. The authors tested formally whether the percentage contribution by genetics to intelligence was less in childhood and adolescence than it was in young adulthood; the answer was 'yes' in both cases. People's genetic inheritance contributes more to intelligence differences after they pass through childhood and adolescence.

The authors' modelling results also indicated that people's differences in environments contributed significantly to their intelligence differences. Both shared and non-shared environment made significant contributions to intelligence differences at all three ages. In Figure 13, find the line for shared environment (C). The shared environment contribution was 33 per cent in childhood, and decreased to 18 per cent in adolescence, and then to 16 per cent in young adulthood. If we identify shared environment mostly with the rearing family, then this suggests that its influence starts by contributing about a third to intelligence differences at about age 9, and lowers to about a sixth by young adulthood. If this appears low, some researchers, using other datasets, find even lower contributions from the shared environment. In Figure 13, the non-shared environment line (E) is quite stable, contributing about a fourth or a fifth to intelligence differences throughout the age range.

Perhaps it seems counter-intuitive that genetic differences increase in their influence on intelligence differences as people grow from children to adults. Or, maybe it is not so surprising. When children are younger, their parents have more oversight of

57

their activities and learning; as they become older, parents have less direct input, and so individuals might be less restrained in expressing their genetic differences. It is also worth having a word about the modest but robust contribution made by non-shared environment. The things that people do and experience that are not shared with a sibling—even an identical twin—matter for people's intelligence differences. However, because this contribution is calculated by its being what is left over when we've taken into account genes and shared environments, we should think about what it represents. Yes, it represents environmental influences not shared in the rearing family, but it also is a sump for other influences, which include measurement error. Traits like intelligence cannot be measured without error, and so it is possible that, if it were measured better, the 'e' element would decrease a bit.

This twin study—actually a combination of various twin studies—has told us that genes and environments matter for people's intelligence differences. By adulthood, about two-thirds of intelligence differences are caused by how people vary in their genetic inheritance. It has also told us that the genetic contribution goes up from childhood to adulthood, and that the effects of shared environments decrease over that period. The answer to the question about how much genes and environments influence intelligence differences is that it depends on age.

Before 2011, that is how the heritability of—the genetic contribution to—intelligence differences was mostly estimated, that is, by using the natural experiment of their being two types of twin pair, one which shares all of the genes, and one which shares half. From the first half of the 20th century onwards there were many twin studies, including some of twins reared apart. Oh, and there were adoption studies too, and studies of various family relationships. The conclusions of these studies were in line with the twin study described above. In 2011, a new method was applied to estimating the heritability of intelligence.

DNA

Twin and adoption studies suggest that genetic differences are important, but they don't tell us which genes contribute. And, however carefully they are done, they will not satisfy some, because they come with assumptions. For example, twin studies assume that the shared environments of monozygotic and dizygotic twins are comparably similar. Although it has not been shown that this is false, there are still some researchers who worry that identical twins' shared environments are more similar than non-identical twins' shared environments, and that this could overestimate the genetic contribution. Well, one can keep arguing within the twin study method, and trying to prove it does not have worrying flaws, or one can do something different. The something different is to go straight to DNA in unrelated people and test that to gain some insight into genetic contributions to intelligence differences.

In 2002, the first 'genome-wide association study' (GWAS) was published. Those who do these types of study refer to it as GWAS (gee-wass; it rhymes with class). That's the type of study that addresses some of the limitations of twin studies. In 2011, my team published the first decent-sized GWAS of intelligence. I now describe what a GWAS is, and then I describe the largest study at the time of writing that has used a GWAS to look at genetic contributions to intelligence differences.

The genetic material is deoxyribonucleic acid (DNA). It is contained in the nucleus of cells. In humans, DNA is chunked into twenty-two pairs of chromosomes and two sex chromosomes: a pair of X chromosomes in females, and an X and a Y chromosome in males. The chemical structure of DNA in a chromosome is a double helix, that is, two intertwined spirals. One gets two of these collections of double helices; one from mother and one from father. The backbone of each helix is a joined-up line of sugar and phosphate molecules. Jutting off each sugar is one of four molecules in a group called nucleotides: adenine (A), thymine (T), cytosine (C), and guanine (G). When facing each other across the two strands of the double helix, A pairs with T, and C pairs with G. These pairings—via chemical attractions which make each pair's members fit together neatly—hold the two strands of the double helix near to each other. In humans, if we count the number of nucleotides along one strand of one pair of the chromosomes, all the way from the start of chromosome 1 to the end of 22 and then along the sex chromosomes, there are about 3 billion (3,000,000,000) of them.

The three billion nucleotide stretch has some structure. Genes are stretches of DNA that code for proteins. There are about 19,000 genes in human DNA. A substantial proportion of human DNA lies outside of genes, though it can still have functions, such as regulating the action of genes. Genes code for proteins. Proteins are made of amino acids. Each amino acid is coded by a combination of three DNA nucleotides.

Not every man or woman has the same stretch of three billion nucleotides. There are differences between people in their DNA. At any one site, there is the commonest nucleotide for a given population. People have a different nucleotide at about one in every thousand places. So, a person is likely to have about four to five million places in their DNA where they differ from the most usual nucleotide for that position. For example, there might be a site on a chromosome where most people have an A, but some people have a C. Because these are nucleotide alternatives in a single place on the DNA strand, they are called single nucleotide polymorphisms (SNPs; it is pronounced snips). Having something other than the usual nucleotide at a particular stretch of DNA can have a variety of effects: it might have no effect; it might be incompatible with life; it might cause an illness; it might affect how one responds to a drug; it might contribute to altering the level of a trait. In total, scientists have found over 100,000,000 SNPs in human studies.

Once it became clear that people's genetic differences consisted to a substantial extent in which SNPs their DNA contained, scientists started trying to ask this question: how does having one SNP versus another at a given position on a chromosome affect humans? How do SNPs relate to variation in health and traits like height and body mass index? Before giving the answer to that, it is necessary to describe the kit involved in testing people's SNPs.

If we are to test how someone's DNA relates to their intelligence, we first need some DNA. A commonly used source of DNA is blood, where it is obtained from the nuclei of the white blood cells. Mouthwashes or cheek swabs may be used, where DNA is obtained from the cells of the cheek (buccal cells) and the mouth. When I paid for the first SNPs to be tested from my participants' blood, in the late 1990s, it cost me about £10 per SNP. We tested just a few at a time. After that, the technology developed, so that thousands of SNPs could be tested together in an array on a chip that was about the size of an 8 g Refresher chew. When my group did our first GWAS study around 2010, we tested 610,000 SNPs in each participant at a cost of about £300 per person, that is, less than a twentieth of a UK penny per SNP. In early 2019 one could buy an array of more than 665,000 SNPs for £28. The cost of testing someone's genetic variations has plummeted.

One does not need to test all of a person's SNPs. In many cases, having one particular SNP makes it more likely that someone will have some other SNPs. Therefore, based on those likelihoods, one can infer far more of a person's genetic make-up than is actually tested. I now describe our findings that used DNA SNP testing to examine genetic contributions to intelligence.

DNA from 300,000 people in fifty-seven studies

Our report, headed by Gail Davies, examined the intelligence and DNA SNPs of 300,486 people. The participants were the combined efforts of fifty-seven studies from Europe, North America, and Australia. All participants had European ancestry. The largest individual study was UK Biobank, which contributed just over half of the participants. For the UK Biobank participants, the intelligence test used was a thirteen-item test of verbal and numerical reasoning. For the other fifty-six samples, the participants had taken at least three different cognitive tests. From these scores, a general intelligence ('g') score was calculated. Each person's DNA was tested at hundreds of thousands of locations. Because having one SNP is closely related to having some other SNPs, the study was able to report on almost 13 million SNPs. The following results arise from having information on DNA variation and intelligence test scores on these almost-third-of-a-million people.

The main results of the study are shown in Figure 14. The contributors to this figure were the 300,486 people from the fifty-seven studies. Along the bottom of the figure there are the twenty-two chromosomes. The X and Y chromosomes were not tested. Up the left-hand side of the figure is the log to the base 10 of the probability value of each SNP's being associated with intelligence; I am going to explain what that means. If one understands what a single dot means in this figure, then the rest follows. In the figure, look at a single dot, any one. Each one represents a SNP; that is, each dot represents a DNA nucleotide point on the chromosome indicated. The height of the dot is how strongly the genetic variation at that nucleotide position is associated with people's intelligence test scores. Each dot's height represents the probability value of the strength of the association between variation on that individual DNA position on that chromosome and intelligence test score.

General cognitive function: SNP-based results

14. This is a Manhattan plot. It is called that because of its 'skyline' appearance. This image has the results of testing the association between DNA differences and differences in general cognitive function in over 300,000 people. The numbers along the bottom are chromosome numbers. Each dot is a genetic variant, a single nucleotide polymorphism; there are millions of them here. The numbers up the left-hand side represent the strengths of association; those above the upper horizontal grey line are statistically significant. There are 148 places on the genome that have significant associations with general cognitive function.

There are 12,987,183 dots on Figure 14. Psychologists often apply a probability value of 0.05 when asking if associations are significant. That is, they live with the possibility that these results occur in one out of twenty studies when there is no true association. If that probability value were applied here, where almost 13 million associations are being run, then one in 20 of the dots could appear to be significant, but would be due to chance. That is unacceptable. The upper of the two horizontal grey lines in Figure 14 shows the level at which the probability value must occur for a dot to be considered significant. It is 5×10^{-8}. That means that each dot's (SNP's) result had to have a probability of occurring by chance of 5 times in 100,000,000. Each dot above the upper horizontal grey line, therefore, is a DNA location where people show differences and for which we can reasonably confidently say that these differences in the DNA are related to intelligence test score differences. There are 11,600 significant SNPs, that is, that number of single nucleotide genetic variants that are related to intelligence test scores. Because the possession of a SNP is related to having others, we asked how many of these were independent SNPs; there were 434. These occurred in 148 regions along the 22 chromosomes. By no means all of these were in regions of DNA that code for genes.

We next did another analysis with the same participants' information. This time, instead of looking at associations between individual SNPs and intelligence, we asked whether variations of the SNPs across whole genes were associated with intelligence. We tested 18,264 genes. SNP variations in 709 of these genes were related to intelligence.

The crude summary this far is that: there are lots of single places in the DNA where people's genetic differences are related to differences in intelligence test scores. There are many genes in which differences are related to intelligence test scores. Intelligence is therefore a polygenic trait, that is, associated with a great many genetic variants in many genes, and in many DNA locations that are not in genes.

The reader is now nudged to ask two questions: first, how much of people's variation in intelligence was accounted for by all these DNA differences?; second, what do these DNA variations and genes do? The answer to the first is given below. The answer to the second is that some of these DNA SNP variations had been related, in other studies, to height, weight, body mass index, lung cancer, Crohn's disease, bipolar disorder, schizophrenia, autism, Parkinson's disease, and Alzheimer's dementia. Genetic variants related to intelligence appear, therefore, to be associated with health. When looking at the sets of genes that were associated with intelligence, several were related to the development of nerve cells and the nervous system.

Back to that first question. We asked what proportion of variation in intelligence test scores is accounted for by SNPs. We did this in two ways. First, we looked at this in some of the individual samples of the fifty-seven contributing studies. I will now describe the largest of these, one of the UK Biobank's sub-samples with 86,010 people in it. The people are unrelated; their DNA was compared to make sure that no one was closer than about a third cousin. Each person is tested for hundreds of thousands of DNA SNPs. Even though these people are unrelated, some have slightly more genetic similarity—based on the hundreds of thousands of SNPs—than others. We used a method that looked at all the 86,010 people and asked the question: to what extent is people's similarity on the hundreds of thousands of DNA SNPs related to their similarity in intelligence? The answer was that, taking into account all tested SNPs, about 25 per cent of people's differences in intelligence test scores were accounted for by DNA SNP differences. This value is called the SNP-based heritability. Note that this estimate is lower than the heritability estimate from twins, above. That is probably because there are rarer genetic variants—not tested here—that contribute to people's intelligence differences. There are other types of genetic variation that were not tested; these, too, could contribute to intelligence differences.

The second way to answer the first question is to use polygenic scores. To do this, we dropped out some of the larger studies from the fifty-seven cohorts, and reran the GWAS. We used the results of this GWAS to ask if we could predict people's intelligence in each study that was dropped out, solely based on DNA information. What we did was use the DNA SNP results from the GWAS to make a genetic score—it is called a polygenic score—in the dropped-out sample. That is, it uses only the dropped-out sample's participants' DNA to ask what their intelligence score should look like based on the GWAS's results. The answer was that up to about 5 per cent of the variation in intelligence in the dropped-out samples were accounted for by the polygenic score. Thus, some prediction of people's differences in intelligence can be made from DNA testing alone. Five per cent is not large, but this will improve as the number of people in the GWAS used to make the polygenic scores increases. However, this would be all but useless for predicting a single person's intelligence test score.

What have we learned about the genetic contributions to intelligence from this GWAS study? First, there are large numbers of genetic variants in large numbers of genes, and many genetic variants outside of genes, that are related to people's intelligence differences. Probably, the number of genetic variants related to intelligence differences in humans is many thousands. Second, the heritability of intelligence based on SNPs is about half of that found using twin studies; that gap will probably be less when more types of genetic variation are studied. Third, using only people's DNA we can predict by better than chance their intelligence differences, but the prediction is not strong. By looking at the progress of GWAS studies for other traits (such as height and body mass index) and illnesses (such as type 2 diabetes and hypertension) we can expect, when the intelligence studies get even larger, there to be far more genetic variants associated with intelligence, and for the prediction to get better, though probably never strong. The SNP-based heritability is unlikely to change much, until genetic variants other than SNPs are studied;

these include rarer genetic variants, and how many copies people have of short strings of DNA.

For researchers there are pluses and minuses from this work. Much has been discovered about the association between DNA variation and intelligence. However, how scientists will deal with the huge number of DNA variants that are related to intelligence is not clear. Each of those variants has only a tiny, tiny effect. How they, together, contribute to intelligence differences and help to write a part of a mechanistic story about cleverness is currently beyond our ken. Researchers and others need urgently to address the ethical issues regarding prediction of intelligence from DNA. Even though such prediction is not good, people will probably try to do it. There is work to do concerning the contributions of types of DNA variation other than SNPs to intelligence differences.

A positive finding from this research was the discovery that the genetic differences that contribute to intelligence differences are also related to other traits and illnesses. To examine this further, we used genetic correlation. This asks how strongly two traits' genetic overlap is. That is, we can use a correlation to express the extent to which the same genetic variants contribute to people's differences in two traits. It is crucial to understand that we used our genetic results on intelligence and then went out and found genetic correlations with other research groups' results from other traits and illnesses; those other traits and illnesses did not need to be assessed in our own samples. In our study there were positive genetic correlations between intelligence and hand grip strength (0.09), lung function (0.19), short-sightedness (0.32), birth weight (0.11), age at menopause (0.13), autism spectrum disorder (0.12; yes, this was positive), brain volume (0.27), and longevity (0.17). Take two examples from this long list: brain volume and longevity. These results mean that some of the same genetic variants that are related to larger brains are also related to being cleverer. The same can be said for being clever and living longer. There were significant negative genetic correlations with

67

hypertension (−0.15), body mass index (−0.13), smoking (−0.20), heart attack (−0.17), lung cancer (−0.26), osteoarthritis (−0.24), attention deficit hyperactivity disorder (−0.37), Alzheimer's disease (−0.37), schizophrenia (−0.23), major depressive disorder (−0.30), the personality trait neuroticism (−0.16), low health satisfaction (−0.26), sleeplessness (−0.12), and long-sightedness (−0.21). Therefore, understanding the genetic contributions to intelligence is not separate from understanding the genetic contributions to physical and mental health. Some of the genetic variants that relate to high intelligence also relate to having a healthier body and lower risks for physical and mental illnesses.

The genetic research on intelligence that uses DNA samples has at least two drivers. The first is to understand why some people are brighter than others, and genetics is part of that. So far, it seems that intelligence differences are influenced by many thousands of genetic variants, each of which has a tiny effect. Given this complexity, the prospect of understanding intelligence differences can appear gloomy. However, some methods used in the DNA-based studies try to understand the gene systems involved in intelligence differences, that is, the systems to which the genetic variants contribute. These studies also help by meshing the genetics of intelligence with, for example, the genetic influences on brain structure and health.

The second driver is prediction. It was made clear above that, given the availability of people's DNA, one can make a better-than-chance prediction of their intelligence differences. However, the best prediction than can be done still does not account for even 10 per cent of people's intelligence differences. Predicting any individual's intelligence from their DNA would be very inaccurate.

I think it is a pity that it was not possible to say more about the environmental contributions. Twin studies, especially, point to there being important environmental influences on intelligence. However, these are often inferred from what is left over when genetic influences have been calculated. It has not proved easy to identify and measure specific environmental influences for the normal range of human intelligence differences. One problem that affects research on environmental influences on children's intelligence can be that some of the measurements—for example, the number of books in the home—are clearly influenced by the parents' behaviours, and the parents are usually genetically related to the children. On the other hand, outside of the typical settings of the genetic/environmental studies on intelligence—that is, non-pathological settings in the higher-income countries—there are more identifiable environmental influences on intelligence. For example researchers such as David Bellinger have addressed the potential cognitive influence of factors such as lead exposure, methylmercury, fluoride and manganese in drinking water, childhood anaesthesia and surgery, concussion, maternal B12 deficiency in pregnancy, exposure to polyfluoroalkyls, congenital heart disease, and others. In the further reading I refer the reader to the report by Aaron Reuben and colleagues from the Dunedin study which found that blood lead levels in childhood were associated with lower intelligence in early middle age.

Heritability—the genetic contributions to differences in a population—is not fixed or universal. The results found apply to the specific sample that was measured. In the USA, the heritability of intelligence appears to be higher among more affluent social classes; thus, intelligence differences are more dependent on the environment among people with more social disadvantage.

Genetic studies raise ethical issues, and there are new ones in DNA-based studies. The necessary discussions should involve well-informed people from as many relevant groups as possible.

Chapter 5
Are smarter people faster?

What are the foundations of people's intelligence differences? By that, I don't mean just environments and genes. A long-standing idea is that people who do well on intelligence tests might be better at some basic psychological processes. Among those supposedly basic processes is mental speed, which is also called processing speed. Smarter people might have faster brains, and their intelligence might follow from that. Sometimes an analogy is made with the processing speed of computers; computers with faster processors can work out complex problems more efficiently, and perhaps more correctly.

There are different ways to measure processing speed. We saw tests of processing speed in Chapter 1, such as Symbol Search, Coding, and Cancellation from the Wechsler Adult Intelligence Scale. We saw in Chapter 2 how these tests of processing speed age impressively (badly) compared with other cognitive domains. Processing speed tests don't involve much thinking. If people are given as much time as they need to answer the individual items, it's unlikely that anyone would make many or any errors. Scores on processing speed tests correlate quite strongly with each other and also with the other Wechsler tests. This tells us that people who do well on the other, more complex, types of cognitive tests also do well on apparently simple tests of processing speed. However, even these speed tests with quite simple questions still have a fair amount going on in them. To answer some of these simple processing speed questions can take over a second or more. For a long time, researchers have looked for something to measure processing speed that is even simpler, and which might be more helpful in understanding what contributes to differences in general intelligence. For over a century, reaction time has been used as a measure of processing speed.

I know this is a bit of a spoiler for the results to come, but I think it is worth signalling. I still find it surprising that people who do well on the sorts of complex tests of thinking that we saw in the Wechsler scales should also do well on quite simple-looking tests, such as reaction time; for example, this might just be pressing a button as fast as possible when a light comes on. Why would that relate to all the thinking skills needed in the different Wechsler tests, and to the overall IQ score? If there is a correlation between a simple speed test and intelligence, it is interesting. However, correlations provide something that still needs to be explained, not an explanation. If we do find a correlation between intelligence test scores and reaction time, we are allowed to say a brief 'ah, that's interesting'. However, we then have to ask ourselves how much we know about reaction time if it is, in turn, expected to explain some of people's intelligence differences.

The West of Scotland Twenty-07 Study

In this study, Geoff Der and I reported the correlation between reaction time and intelligence. It is the only such study in a large sample of people who are representative of their background population. It also has decent, if short, tests of intelligence and reaction time.

The Twenty-07 Study was named that way because it started in 1987 and was planned to end after twenty years, in 2007. It recruited people from in and around Glasgow, Scotland's largest city. The participants were, at the start of the study, aged 15, 35, or

55 years old. Therefore, one can calculate that, after twenty years of follow-up, the two younger groups would reach the age that the next one above them had been at the start of the study. The overall aim of the study was to find out more about the health differences between the social classes across the adult life course. The data we used to study intelligence and reaction time came from wave four of the Twenty-07 Study, which took place in 2000 and 2001. At that time, the three groups were aged 30, 50, and 69 years old. The number of people who had full data for analysis was 714, 813, and 669 for the three age groups, respectively.

The participants took a test of their reaction time. The device used is shown in Figure 15. The rectangle at the top left is a liquid crystal display where numbers appear when the test is running. It is also used, later, by the tester, to see the results. The start button is used by the tester to start the test. There are five response buttons at the bottom, with the numbers—from left to right—1, 2,

15. A device for testing simple reaction time and four-choice reaction time.

0, 3, and 4 beside them. These are used by the participant to make responses.

Two types of reaction time are tested: simple and choice. In the simple reaction time test, the participant places their chosen finger lightly on the '0' key. Their instruction is: 'as soon as a "0" appears on the screen, press the "0" key down as quickly as you can'. There are eight practice trials and twenty test trials. A person's simple reaction time is the mean of those twenty test trials, and is calculated in milliseconds. People show large differences in their means, but a typical time for a single trial is around a third of a second. This is a much shorter time than it takes to complete any item from, say, the Wechsler scales.

In the choice reaction time test, the participant has to press the correct key to match a number that appears on the small screen. The participant places four fingers lightly on the '1', '2', '3', and '4' keys. Usually, it is the index and middle fingers of both hands. One number appears at a time; it can be 1, 2, 3, or 4. Their instruction is: 'as soon as you see a number, press the correct key as quickly as you can, and try not to make mistakes'. Unlike the simple reaction time test, it is possible to make errors in choice reaction time. However, few people make many errors. There are eight practice trials and forty test trials. A person's choice reaction time is the mean of their correct responses in those forty test trials, and is calculated in milliseconds. A typical time is around two-thirds of a second, about twice as long as simple reaction time. This is still a lot shorter than the time it takes to answer a question in a typical intelligence test.

The intelligence test used in the Twenty-07 Study was part 1 of the Alice Heim 4 test. It has some practice items. The test proper has sixty-five questions, and a time limit of 10 minutes. There are about the same numbers of verbal and numerical reasoning questions. The types of question involve analogical reasoning, vocabulary, mental arithmetic, and completing logical series.

The Alice Heim 4 test and the reaction time tests present very different types of task. Individual items in the simple and choice reaction time tasks are done in a fraction of a second, and there is almost no intellectual content to the tasks. Although someone might occasionally rush a response in a choice reaction time task and press the wrong number, if they were allowed to take their time they would not make errors. Compare that with the Alice Heim 4 test, whose items take several-to-many seconds to answer, and in which there are some questions that some people would not answer correctly, no matter how long they were given. Yet, we will now see that people who do well on the Alice Heim 4 test of general intelligence also tend to have faster reaction times.

Figure 16 shows the results. Look at the lower panels first, which are for choice reaction time (CRT). Each circle on the figure represents a person. Along the horizontal is how well they scored on the Alice Heim 4 test, out of 65. Up the left-hand side is the average time it took to respond in the reaction time test. How high their circle is represents their average choice reaction time, in thousandths of a second. Therefore, 1,000 is a second. The bottom right-hand panel is for the 669 69-year-olds, born in the 1930s. The cloud of dots generally goes from top left to bottom right; that is, people with better Alice Heim 4 intelligence test scores tend to have shorter (better) choice reaction times. The correlation is −0.53, which is a strong association. In Figure 16, the lower-middle cloud of circles has the results for the 50-year-olds, and the lower left-hand one is for the 30-year-olds. The cloud of circles sits lower in the box as one moves from the oldest group to the youngest one; that is, younger people, overall, have shorter (better) reaction times. That should not be a surprise, after what we saw in Chapter 2. The 30-year-olds' mean choice reaction time is 539 milliseconds, the 50-year-olds' mean is 623 milliseconds, and the 69-year-olds' mean is 729 milliseconds. The two younger groups also show a tendency for their clouds of circles to go from top left to bottom right. For the 50-year-olds, the correlation between the Alice Heim 4 general intelligence test and choice

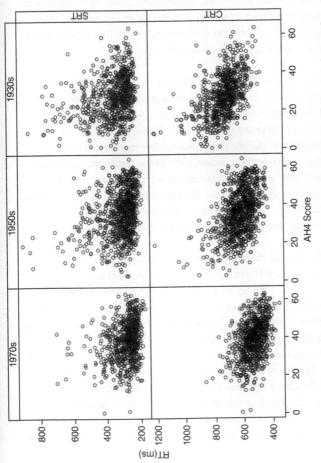

16. This shows the association between intelligence and simple and choice reaction time for people aged 30 years (born in the 1970s), 50 (born in the 1950s), and 69 (born in the 1930s). Along the bottom is the score on the Alice Heim 4 test of general intelligence. Up the left-hand side is the reaction time in milliseconds for simple reaction time (upper row), and choice reaction time (lower row).

reaction time is −0.47. For the 30-year-olds, the correlation is −0.44. These are medium-sized correlations. In summary, in large samples of people who are representative of the Glasgow and the surrounding area's population in Scotland, choice reaction time is negatively correlated, at medium to strong levels, with a general intelligence test of verbal and numerical reasoning. This holds for people from young adulthood to older age.

The top three panels in Figure 16 show the results for simple reaction time versus the Alice Heim 4 general intelligence test. Recall that simple reaction time involves just pressing a button whenever a '0' appears on the screen. There is no choice of response button. As one might expect, because there's less thinking needed and no choice, each of the three groups' simple reaction times are shorter (faster) than their choice reaction times. For the 69-year-olds in the top right panel, the mean simple reaction time is 354 milliseconds. For the 50-year-olds it is 318 milliseconds. For the 30-year-olds it is 290 milliseconds.

We'll first look at the top-right panel, which is the association between the Alice Heim 4 general intelligence test and simple reaction time for the 69-year-olds. Before that, almost close your eyes and peer at the lower three panels. You will see that they make quite clean ellipses, slanted from top-left to bottom-right. However, the top-right panel is a less clean ellipse. There is more vertical scatter of points at the lower Alice Heim 4 scores than at the higher scores. There's no such marked tendency for the panel below that, that is, the choice reaction time one for the same group. For the bottom-right panel, as you move from high to low Alice Heim 4 scores, the circles show much the same amount of vertical scatter. In the top-right panel, the word for this difference in vertical scatter of points going from high Alice Heim 4 scores to lower ones is heteroscedasticity. I know, I know, it sounds very abstruse, but I am comforted to know that something like this has a specific word. It'll make you sound smart if you ever get the chance to use it. It does sound complicated, but it is also interesting. It means that, in this group of 69-year-olds, the simple reaction times of people with lower Alice Heim 4 scores are not just slower on average, they are also more variable. People with lower general intelligence differ more in their simple reaction times than do people with higher intelligence, as well as having longer (slower, worse) simple reaction times on average. This difference in simple reaction time scatter—heteroscedasticity—is there also in the 50-year-olds (upper middle panel) and in the 30-year-olds (upper left panel), though it is less pronounced than in the oldest group.

In summary, the relationship between simple reaction time and intelligence is not as straightforward as that between choice reaction time and intelligence. But there is still some significant association. For the 69-year-olds the correlation between simple reaction time and Alice Heim 4 general intelligence is –0.32. For the 50-year-olds it is –0.30. For the 30-year-olds it is –0.27. These are medium-sized correlations. To me, these correlations are still surprising; why would the time it takes to press a button when a zero appears relate to the score on a complicated intelligence test?

We have learned here that there are large to medium correlations between intelligence test scores and choice reaction times, and medium-sized correlations with simple reaction times. The correlations appear at all adult ages, including healthy young adults. The correlations are interesting. They tell us that intelligence test scores relate to performance on tests that are not tapping school-based learning, and are unlikely to be surrogates for social advantage. But we must avoid the urge—if it is felt—to declare that we now understand that part of people's intelligence differences can be explained by the brain's processing speed. First, because we don't yet know what reaction time tests in the brain. Second, because we can't assume that reaction time differences cause intelligence differences rather than the reverse.

Now, let's look at a processing speed test that is apparently even simpler, and ask if it is related to intelligence test scores.

The Lothian Birth Cohort 1936

In this study, we measured processing speed using inspection time. Some might make the case that reaction time, especially choice reaction time, does involve a bit of thinking. The person taking the test has to identify the number on the screen, then decide which response key needs to be chosen to indicate that, and then execute the correct choice as fast as possible while trying not to make an error. Even if we could answer that potential objection by saying that the responses are made in about half to two-thirds of a second, and so not much thinking could happen, let's take it seriously and ask if performance on anything that's apparently simpler is associated with intelligence. Inspection time meets that criterion.

The results here were from 987 participants with relevant data from the Lothian Birth Cohort 1936. They were mentioned in Chapter 2. Their mean age at testing was 69.6 years, with little variation because they were all born in the same year. To assess general intelligence, a summary score from the following subtests of the Wechsler Adult Intelligence Scale was used: Matrix Reasoning, Letter-number Sequencing, Block Design, Coding, and Symbol Search. These tests were described in Chapter 1.

To understand what is involved in the inspection time task, have a look at Figure 17. The participant sits in front of a computer screen in a room with a controlled amount of light. Here is what is involved in doing each inspection time item; it is illustrated by following Figure 17 from left to right. First, a small cross appears in the middle of the computer screen. This is the cue to 'get ready'. Next, a stimulus appears; it is two vertical lines of markedly different lengths, joined at the top with a crossbar. This takes one of two forms, which is why there are two rows in Figure 17. One form of the stimulus has a long line on the left and a short line on the right; the alternative form has the long line on the right and

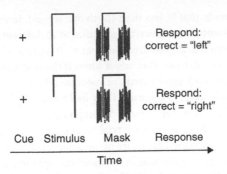

17. The sequence of events for an item in the inspection time test. There are two different stimuli. The top row shows the temporal sequence when the stimulus has the long line on the left. The bottom row shows the temporal sequence when the stimulus has the long line on the right.

the short line on the left. Immediately after the stimulus is taken away, a 'mask' appears. Its job is to wipe away the after-image of the stimulus. It prevents the effect that is seen if one switches a light on in a dark room and then off again; one 'sees' the room after the light has gone off. After the mask is turned off, the participant makes a response to tell the researcher whether the stimulus's long line was on the right or on the left. There is no hurry; the participant is asked to take their time in responding. Their reaction time is not tested; all the researcher records is whether the participant indicated the location of the long line correctly or not. If the stimulus is shown for a long time, say a fifth of a second or more, people don't make errors. So far, the task involved in this test is trivially easy. Next, I explain how the task is implemented, so that differences in people's performances will emerge.

The key to the inspection time task is that the long line–short line stimulus is shown for different amounts of time. In easy trials, it is shown for 200 milliseconds, that is, a fifth of a second. In the hardest trials, the stimulus is shown to the participant for only

6 milliseconds, that is, less than 150th of a second. In this study, the participants were shown the stimulus at 15 different durations, ranging from 6 to 200 milliseconds, with 10 repeats of each. During those 150 trials, they never knew if the next trial would have a long (easy), short (hard), or medium stimulus duration. The test took about 15 minutes. They had a good deal of practice before taking the test in earnest. To emphasize, they did not respond quickly—the way each trial is set up, they are not able to; they simply responded at leisure by pressing a left or right button, to indicate whether the long line was on the right or on the left. The inspection time task asks the question: how much information can a person take in when a stimulus is flashed in front of their eyes for a brief time?

The inspection time task involves no speeded responding. It requires the simplest of decisions—indicating whether a long line was on the right or left—based on a discrimination that does not have errors when the stimulus is shown for about a fifth of a second. If one looks at the chance of getting the left–right decision correct as a function of the stimulus duration, it increases steadily from chance to near-to-perfect as stimulus duration goes from brief to long exposures. When the two lines are shown for about 30 milliseconds or less, people's responses were close to chance; they couldn't spot where the long line was when they were flashed up too briefly. When the two lines were shown for longer than about 100 milliseconds, the responses were close-to-always correct. Remember that the participant never knew what the next duration would be—easy, medium, or hard—and so the fact that almost everyone got the easy ones correct was a good check on the fact that attention does not waver. The ascent from chance to near-perfect responding as the exposure times go from short to long is smooth when the overall performance of the group was examined.

People showed differences in how good they were at doing the inspection time task. In the 150 trials, some people scored better than others. Note that one would get about 75 correct by guessing. The differences in people's performance were not due to visual acuity. The difference between the long and short lines of the stimulus is large. Those people whose data were analysed were able to perform almost perfectly on the easy trials. It seems, then, that when people have a brief stimulus flashed in front of them, some people extract more and better information from it than others can. Is this capability related to intelligence?

In this study, 987 of the Lothian Birth Cohort 1936 completed the inspection time test and the Wechsler Adult Intelligence Scale tests. The correlation between intelligence test scores and inspection time scores was 0.32. People who had higher intelligence test scores tended to make more correct decisions about the inspection time stimuli. More intelligent people, therefore, tended to pick up more information from those briefly presented visual stimuli.

Speed and other cognitive processes

The surprising link between quite simple skills of processing speed and higher-level thinking is potentially the start of a trail that could give part of the answer to what it means to be clever. The correlations between intelligence and reaction time and inspection time are a response to those who would dismiss intelligence tests as based on social class, or just academic book-learning. It is hard to maintain those criticisms when one looks at the content of reaction time and inspection time tests. Overall, though, this field is characterized by many researchers working on many different tests of processing speed, which makes it difficult to synthesize the work. For each test of processing speed that correlates substantially with intelligence test scores, we'd want to know why, and that is an awful lot of not-yet-being-done follow-up work.

And there is a broader difficulty. Speed is not the only psychological process to which researchers look for an explanation of intelligence differences. There are lively research efforts to try to understand intelligence differences in terms of working memory (we saw a test of that in Chapter 1) and also executive function. I encourage the reader to read about them, but with reservations. Working memory tends to be assessed with tests that are very like intelligence tests; therefore, I am not sure how much explaining is being done there. One encouraging thing about processing speed tests is how little they resemble typical intelligence tests. And executive function tends to be assessed by a mix of tests, some of which relate to each other and some not, and so it is hard to accept that it provides a coherent set of processes that lie under intelligence differences rather than just reflect some of them.

So far, we have seen genetic and environmental contributions to intelligence differences, and perhaps contributions from processing speed. Next, let's look at the brain.

Chapter 6
What do more intelligent brains look like?

This chapter is about measures of human brains using brain-imaging techniques. There are types of imaging that study the brain's structure. They can tell us how much of different types of brain tissue a person has, and can indicate how healthy some brain tissue is. There are types of brain imaging that study the blood-flow changes when the brain is doing a mental task. These are functional brain-imaging studies. There are types of brain imaging that examine the electrical activity of the brain at rest and in response to stimuli. These are electroencephalographic (EEG, or brain waves) and brain evoked response methods. There are types of brain imaging that examine the magnetic activity that comes about because of the electrical activity of the brain. These are magnetoencephalography (MEG) methods.

In this chapter I focus on structural brain imaging. I think that the clearest, as-yet-most-reproducible associations between brain measures and intelligence test scores come from that type of imaging.

The Lothian Birth Cohort 1936

Stuart Ritchie in my team headed this study. It is an unusually large single sample for this type of study, and it assesses a range of aspects of brain structure.

The people tested are from the Lothian Birth Cohort 1936. We heard about them in Chapters 2 and 5. The present study is from their second wave of testing in older age, when they were about 73 years old. Of the 1,091 who we recruited at the age of about 70 years, 886 came back for testing at age 73. Of these, 700 were willing and able to take a magnetic resonance imaging structural brain scan; 672 of them provided usable brain-imaging and cognitive test data for this study.

The participants of the Lothian Birth Cohort 1936 took fifteen cognitive tests. They included tests of memory, of non-verbal and spatial reasoning, of processing speed, and of knowledge. Many of the cognitive tests came from the Wechsler Intelligence and Wechsler Memory Scales. They also took the reaction time and inspection time tests described in Chapter 5. From the scores on the fifteen tests, each person obtained a general cognitive factor—general intelligence, 'g'—score. The idea was to test the strength of the correlation between this general intelligence score and different measures of brain structure.

To obtain brain measures, the participants had a brain scan in a magnetic resonance imaging (MRI) scanner that lasted about seventy-five minutes. This type of scanner uses strong magnetic fields to excite hydrogen atoms in water-containing parts of the body, including the brain. By doing so, it is able to plot and measure different types of structure in the brain. This is because the different tissues' hydrogen atoms return to their non-excited states at different rates.

I don't think it is necessary to say much more than that about MRI scanning to understand the present study. What is important to understand is that the last few decades have seen considerable advances in what structural MRI scanning can measure about brains. Here are the main brain measurements we took from the Lothian Birth Cohort 1936 participants. There are four of them, as illustrated in Figure 18.

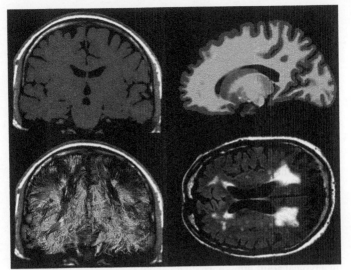

18. **Anonymized brain scans from the Lothian Birth Cohort 1936.**
These images indicate total brain volume (top left; coronal plane slice),
brain cortical thickness (top right; saggital plane slice), brain white
matter connections (bottom left; coronal plane slice), and
hyperintensities (like scars) in the brain's white matter (bottom right;
axial plane slice).

Total brain volume: This was obtained by first measuring the total
volume inside the inner layer of the skull and then subtracting the
cerebrospinal fluid. The cerebrospinal fluid is the liquid that
bathes the brain inside the skull. MRI scanning is able to tell apart
this fluid from brain tissues. Total brain volume, then, tells us how
much brain, of any type of tissue, sits inside the skull. Our
hypothesis was that people scoring higher on intelligence tests
tend to have bigger brains.

Brain cortical thickness: The outer surface of the brain's two
hemispheres is called the cortex. This is the 'grey matter' one hears
about. It is largely the brain cells, especially the nerve cells of the
brain: the neurons. The cortex is heavily folded. It is between

85

2 and 3 millimetres thick. MRI scanning is able to separate brain tissue into grey matter and white matter (see below). Therefore, an average cortical thickness—the thickness of the brain's grey matter—was calculated from measurements at 81,924 points on each person's brain. Our hypothesis was that people scoring higher on intelligence tests have thicker brain cortices, indicating more grey matter.

Brain white matter integrity (or health): The white matter of the brain lies mostly below the grey matter of the cortex. The white matter is the connecting network of 'wires' in the brain. Some of the connections are long, and some are short. The connections are the axons, which are fibres that emerge from nerve cells and connect to other nerve cells. White matter is called 'white' because these connecting fibres have an insulating layer of a white-looking fatty material called myelin. The total length of all the connections in a typical adult human would go about four times round the circumference of the earth. A type of brain scanning called diffusion MRI can indicate how healthy the white matter is. Consider this analogy to get an idea about how that is done. For messages to flow efficiently along a bundle of white matter axons we want them to be like a bundle of drinking straws with no holes or cracks along their lengths. If there were such holes and cracks, there would be leakage off to the side. The diffusion MRI procedure can test the extent to which connecting bundles of axons in the brain's white matter are like intact bundles of straws or like bundles of straws with cracks and holes along their lengths. Another analogy is with a road network. People will get to where they want to go if all the roads are open, and if the roads are free from lane closures and potholes and other types of damage. Our hypothesis was that people scoring higher on intelligence tests have healthier brain white matter, which is sometimes called better white matter integrity. In this study, the health of the white matter connections was assessed for twelve major white matter bundles in each person's brain; these are the brain's connecting motorways, if you like. People who have healthier brain white matter in one bundle tend to have healthier white matter in other bundles, and so a score of average white matter health/integrity was used.

Brain white matter hyperintensities: Some areas of the brain's white matter show up especially brightly in MRI brain scanning. That is why they are called white matter hyperintensities; they are intensely bright in the brain scan signal they give. These can be thought of as scars in the brain's connections. People tend to pick up more of them as they grow older. They are not an illness per se—lots of healthy people have some of them—though they are found in greater numbers in some illnesses, such as multiple sclerosis. One idea about white matter hyperintensities is that they can occur because of problems with the small blood vessels in the brain. It seems likely that brain communication might be somewhat affected—even in healthy people—if they have more of these white matter 'scars' that could interrupt efficient processing in the brain: their 'straws' are more leaky; their 'road networks' are more disrupted. Our hypothesis was that people scoring higher on intelligence tests have fewer white matter hyperintensities.

Our hypotheses were all supported. Here are the correlations between these four brain measures and general intelligence in the Lothian Birth Cohort 1936 sample:

Total brain volume: correlation with general intelligence ('g') = 0.31. Higher intelligence test scores tend to go with having a larger brain overall. After finding this, Simon Cox in my team looked at the association between general intelligence (formed from four tests) and brain volume in over 8,000 participants (mean age 63 years) in the UK Biobank study. We heard about them in Chapter 3. The correlation was 0.276, that is, similar to the one found in the Lothian Birth Cohort 1936.

Brain cortical thickness: correlation with g = 0.24. Higher intelligence test scores tend to go with having a thicker cerebral cortex overall, that is, having thicker grey matter on the surface of the brain.

Brain white matter integrity: correlation with g = 0.24. Higher intelligence test scores tend to go with having healthier white matter connections overall.

Brain white matter hyperintensities: correlation with g = −0.20. Higher intelligence test scores tend to go with having fewer white matter hyperintensities, that is, having fewer of these 'scars' in the brain's connecting tissue.

People who have higher general intelligence tend, therefore, to have larger brains, thicker grey matter on the surface of the brain, and healthier white matter brain connections. The associations are not strong, but some aspects of brain structure do relate to intelligence test scores.

Brain volume and intelligence

Jakob Pietschnig found eighty-eight studies that had examined the association between intelligence test scores and brain volume. Some were of healthy people. Some were of groups of people with autism, schizophrenia, or brain injury. Almost all of the brain scanning was done using magnetic resonance imaging. The people's ages ranged from childhood to old age. There were 120 correlation coefficients; some studies reported more than one sample. There was an overall correlation of 0.24 between brain volume and general intelligence; people with bigger brains tended to score higher on intelligence tests. The correlation between general intelligence and brain volume was 0.26 in healthy samples, based on 84 correlations.

The authors wrote a long discussion section entitled 'Why is brain size associated with intelligence?' The answer is that they don't know. And neither does anyone else. They speculated about whether bigger brains might have greater numbers of nerve cells, but there are not any sufficiently good studies to substantiate that.

Gilles Gignac and Tim Bates conducted a later meta-analysis on intelligence and brain volume, which re-did Pietschnig's meta-analysis. They took more note of the quality of the intelligence tests. They also left out clinical samples and any samples that included children. This revised meta-analysis is useful in indicating the association between brain volume and general intelligence in healthy adults. Based on these criteria, they found 32 correlations with a total of 1,758 participants. There was an overall correlation of 0.29 between brain volume and general intelligence. They found that there are slightly higher correlations when the intelligence tests used in the study were rated as good or excellent; in these cases, the correlation tended to be above 0.3. They also pointed out that the samples of people included in the studies have a narrower range of intelligence than the full population. This lowers correlations. Therefore, they say, if we were to take into account both this and the fact that some studies do not use very good intelligence tests, the correlation might be higher than the one we find from a basic meta-analysis. Both of these meta-analyses were published before the large-scale UK Biobank data were available, which found an association of 0.276 between brain volume and intelligence. As is obvious, the results are similar.

If I were asked about the correlation between general intelligence and brain volume in healthy adults, I think that it is in the highish 0.2s, or a wee bit higher. I am aware that there are aspects of studies that make that a conservative estimate, but I think that being conservative is better than risking exaggerating the association. That size of correlation is not very strong, but neither is it zero. It is large enough to be quite interesting and to be explained. It hasn't been explained.

Intelligence beyond brain structure

Given the space that was to hand, and given that I think it affords the most robust associations with intelligence, I have emphasized the findings from structural brain imaging, mostly from MRI. However, there are also imaging studies that relate the brain's functional changes to intelligence test scores. These have provided less robust findings, though it has been proposed that the structural and functional imaging findings have some agreed results. As a readable guide to intelligence's relationships with both brain structure and functions—and more—I recommend Richard Haier's book *The Neuroscience of Intelligence*. He is associated with the parieto-frontal integration theory of intelligence (P-FIT). It's the idea that there's a limited network in the brain that has individual differences that underpin some of people's intelligence differences. Whereas I judge the structural imaging studies to be the safe ground to date for brain–intelligence associations, Haier looks further afield, using more-or-less strong findings, and attempts a more integrated account.

In Chapters 4, 5, and 6 we have seen genes, processing speed, and brain structure having significant and modest associations with intelligence, each hinting at the origins of intelligence differences. Each area has left more work to do to understand the associations. Next, rather than causes of intelligence differences, we shall ask about some of their consequences.

Chapter 7
Does intelligence matter in the school and the workplace?

Entire books—popular and scholarly—are available that disparage the invention and applications of intelligence tests. Intelligence tests were sometimes used inappropriately and over-zealously at times during the 20th century, and to the exclusion of other important human characteristics. They are a tool that can be misused. All tools run this risk, but, as Queen Elizabeth I ripostes in Sir Walter Scott's *Kenilworth*, '"it is ill arguing against the use of anything from its abuse".' So, let's ask if intelligence test scores have some utility. We are not asking whether an intelligence test score totally predicts human achievements or outcomes—it never does, or anything near it—just whether intelligence test scores have some predictive power.

The first tests of human intelligence appeared in 1905. They were developed by Alfred Binet and Théodore Simon in Paris. They were given a practical problem: how might the authorities identify and help those children who would not benefit from the normal style of education? IQ-type tests, which now number many hundreds, were their answer. Therefore, what we call tests of intelligence were invented to serve a practical, pro-social purpose.

The main applications of intelligence tests are in education, in the workplace, and in medicine. Thus, mental tests are used to assess mental capability in the settings of school performance, work performance, and in looking at the effects of illnesses and medical treatments on the brain's functions. Where would the assessment of cognitive decline in older age and neurological and other illnesses be without cognitive tests? In Chapter 8, I shall outline the new field of cognitive epidemiology, in which people's intelligence test scores are predictors of health and longevity. Here, we look at education and work.

English National GCSE examination results

Does an intelligence test score predict who will do well in achieving more and better educational qualifications? This question is similar to the first-ever use of intelligence tests. In the United Kingdom, intelligence tests were widely used around the middle two quarters of the 20th century to select children at age 11+ years into longer and more-academic versus shorter and less-academic streams of secondary education. The tests fell out of favour for that purpose, especially as the school leaving age was raised and education became mostly comprehensive. However, under another name and for other purposes, there is still massive use of cognitive testing in United Kingdom schools. They are called 'cognitive ability tests' rather than intelligence tests. They are used, for example, for estimating the value that schools add to their students' national examination results, given the cognitive abilities with which they began. Here, I will ask whether a general intelligence test score at about age 11 predicts how well children will do in national examinations at the age of about 16 years.

The dataset I describe includes the Cognitive Abilities Test (the CAT). We saw the CAT intelligence test battery in Chapter 2; I described its subtests and domains. About a million children sit versions of this test in the United Kingdom each year. In our study, over 70,000 children's results were examined. The CAT data from 1997 were used, from the academic year 1997/8. The children tested were 11 years old. As a group, they were representative of the population of England in the United Kingdom. The CAT's subtests combine to give scores on the cognitive domains of verbal reasoning, quantitative reasoning, and non-verbal reasoning. Children's scores on these domains all correlate highly. Therefore, we computed a general intelligence factor as we saw at the pinnacle of the hierarchy in Chapter 1. The CAT's general intelligence factor accounts for about 70 per cent of the differences among children in the CAT's tests' scores. A combined score of all three of the CAT's domains gives a good measure of general intelligence. Even though there were more than 35,000 boys and girls in this sample, there was no average difference in their general intelligence scores. Girls did better on the verbal reasoning ability domain, by just under 4 points on an IQ scale (with a standard deviation of 15).

We obtained permission to link the 70,000+ children's CAT scores in 1997 to the May 2002 results for the General Certificate of Secondary Education (GCSE) in England. These are national examinations taken by children at age 15 to 16 years, about five years after they took the CAT tests at age 11. The GCSEs have nine levels of score, from lowest to highest. Our study examined the results from twenty-five different GCSE examination subjects. The children came from 973 schools in England. Our sample was more than a fifth of the total English national GCSE dataset for that year. Our study included only the students from mainstream state secondary schools and those who sat the same version of the CAT. The maximum number of children for analysis was 74,403.

We began by asking how the overall general intelligence score from the CAT at age 11 correlated with overall GCSE results at age about 16 years, around five years later. Students sit GCSEs in many subjects. It is common to make a score for each child that is the total of their best eight GCSE results. The correlation between CAT-assessed general intelligence at age 11 and best-eight GCSE total score at age about 16 was 0.72. This is a strong correlation. Not all children sit all GCSE subjects; they choose from the twenty-five. The correlation between the CAT general intelligence score and the commonest two single GCSEs was 0.67 for English, and 0.77 for Mathematics. Every one of the twenty-five GCSEs' scores correlated positively with CAT general intelligence, with eleven having correlations greater than 0.6. Even the lowest correlation—0.43 between CAT general intelligence and Art and Design—was still substantial.

Despite girls and boys having the same average score on CAT-based general intelligence at age 11 years, girls had better scores on 24 of the 25 GCSEs, that is, all except physics, on which boys and girls scored equally. The girls' better performance was not accounted for by their better verbal ability on the CAT. This is important. Girls, in this massive sample, tend to obtain better GCSEs at age 16 for the same general cognitive scores at age 11 than do boys. GCSEs are the entry to the next level of qualifications—the A Levels—which determine university entry and careers. They matter for people's lives.

Let's go back to the CAT–GCSE correlation. To get a truer idea of the correlation between CAT-based general intelligence score at age 11 and GCSE performance at age 16 it is better to study only those students who sat the same GCSEs. Figure 19 shows the

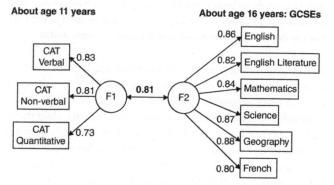

19. The association between children's differences in general cognitive function (F1) at age about 11 years on the Cognitive Abilities Test battery and general GCSE performance (F2) at age about 16 based on the six most-commonly-taken-together set of GCSEs.

results of this analysis. There were 13,248 students who sat GCSEs in English, English Literature, Mathematics, Science, Geography, and French. This was the commonest set of six GCSE topics. Note the three CAT domains, and that they have a high correlation with a circle called F1. This F1 is called a latent trait—the concept on to which the three domains are linked, based on the fact that they are all highly correlated. We will call F1 'CAT-based general intelligence', from age 11. Note the six GCSE topics; they all have high correlations with a latent trait, F2, which is based on the fact that all of the six are highly correlated with each other. We will call F2 'general GCSE performance', from age 16. The statistical procedure I used was structural equation modelling. It's complicated, but never mind that. Its purpose was to create F1 and F2 from the CAT and GCSE scores, respectively, and to estimate the correlation between them. The correlation between general intelligence at age 11 and general GCSE performance at age about 16 years was 0.81. This is high: people's intelligence differences at age 11 are a powerful predictor of their differences in educational outcomes at age 16.

Given that educational outcomes are gate-keepers for entry into follow-on, higher education and to jobs and professions, then this is practically important. If people's intelligence test scores can be optimized by age 11 then it bodes well for their gaining more and better educational credentials later on. We provided a demonstration of that. Gaining five or more GCSEs in the top four scoring bands (A* to C) was used by the UK government's education department to assess school performance. That is a criterion sometimes used for entry to training and more education. Just over 39,000 pupils met this criterion, and over 30,000 did not. Fifty-eight per cent of those who had an average score on CAT general intelligence at age 11 obtained five or more GCSEs from A* to C. Ninety-one per cent of those whose general intelligence was one standard deviation (15 IQ points) higher achieved that criterion. Only 16 per cent of those whose general intelligence was an average of one standard deviation (15 IQ points) lower achieved that criterion.

These are strong results with respect to intelligence as a predictor. However, there was also much variation in children's GCSE performance that was not related to CAT scores. Indeed, we emphasized that the children's intelligence test score differences were accounting for around only half or slightly more of their differences in GCSE scores. Therefore, other factors must make important contributions too. Independently of intelligence test scores, being female and having higher scores on the CAT verbal ability domain were associated with better GCSE results. We could not test for, but we suggested that, other things might contribute to GCSE success; these included school attendance and engagement, personality traits, motivation, effort, parental support, teaching quality, school ethos, etc. Intelligence is not close to being the whole story of educational success in this context, but it is a substantial part of it.

Job selection and job performance

After school, do intelligence test scores predict who will perform well in the workplace? The work-related dataset I shall refer to is a large compilation of findings by the late John Hunter, with his research colleagues Ronda Hunter and Frank Schmidt. Their interests were in job selection, in finding the right people to do a job well. They asked the following simple-seeming question: is it worthwhile for an employer to select people for a job on the basis of, among other things, a test of general mental ability (general intelligence)? The emphasis here is not on each of the individuals offering themselves for selection. Rather, the focus is on those making the selection, and it is centred on a practical problem. Imagine that an employer wishes to select people to begin new jobs in their workplace. What is the best method of selecting the most productive new staff? How can they tell who will bring the most benefit to their organization? In essence, among the criteria that they compile in their selection portfolio, would it be worthwhile having a test of general mental ability?

Hunter and his colleagues made a speciality of meta-analysis. The area that they meta-analysed is decision-making in job hiring. They pored through studies conducted over eighty-five years of psychological research. They read and filleted thousands of studies to form their conclusions. They compiled a comprehensive guide to what is best in selecting for job performance. Though their research papers can be quite technical and bristling with statistics, they have a strong and simple message. Hiring decisions matter: they can make or lose a lot of money. It is important in hiring to have some set of open and fair criteria for selection that relate as highly as possible to how well the person will do the job. That's the key, then: what are the best ways of selecting people to do a job well?

John Hunter and Frank Schmidt examined the relative predictive power of nineteen different ways of selecting people for jobs. Everything from interviews, through intelligence testing, and having people try out the job, to examining the applicants' handwriting (a popular method, then, in France and Israel especially). There's a selected summary of these results in Figure 20; the diagram represents the cumulative knowledge from almost a century of research and thousands of research studies.

Each of the columns in Figure 20 represents a different way of hiring people, that is, they are selection methods. The length of the column represents the size of the correlation between people's rankings on each selection method and later performance on the job. The longer the column, the stronger is this relation, and the better is the method of selection. The longest column belongs to work sample tests. This is where one can get all of the applicants actually to do the job for a time and assess how efficient they are. These are costly to set up and the majority of jobs do not lend themselves to this type of procedure. Note, too, that highly

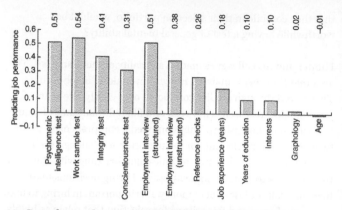

20. **Some factors that were tested for their association with job performance. The longer the column, the better the prediction. The numbers are correlation coefficients.**

structured employment interviews do relatively well, but the more typical unstructured interviews are poorer. Reference checks on their own are not especially helpful. Years of job experience and years of education do not do a good job of predicting people's performance in doing the job. Age is uninformative. Graphology, the analysis of handwriting, tells nothing about how well the person will do the job. Not only is selection by this method losing people money in making sub-optimal selection decisions, the cost of having it done is wasted too. It is unfair, because it ends up rejecting people for something that is entirely unrelated to their ability to do the job.

In Figure 20, the column for the general intelligence/psychometric test is comparatively long, almost as good as the best predictors of job performance. It does offer some useful information about how well people, on average, will do the job in many types of employment. Unlike other selection methods, it can be applied nearly universally. It can be given for jobs where it is not possible to do a job try-out or compose a highly structured interview. Compared to most other methods, the general mental ability test is quick, cheap, and convenient. It has the lowest cost of any of the relatively good methods. Looking over the research literature, there is much more evidence for the success of the general mental ability test than any other method of selection. It has been used in many more research studies than any other method.

Tests of general intelligence have other merits in the job selection process. They are the best predictors of which employees will learn most as they progress on the job. They are the best predictors of who will benefit most from training programmes. However, the power of the general intelligence test to predict job success is not equal for all types of job. The more professional, the more mentally complex the job is, the more successfully the mental test score will predict the success on the job. Therefore, mental tests do poorest in unskilled jobs and are better at predicting success on professional and skilled jobs. In their research report Schmidt and Hunter concluded that, 'Because of its special status, GMA [tests of general mental ability or general intelligence] can be considered the primary personnel measure for hiring decisions, and one can consider the remaining 18 as supplements to GMA measures.'

Hunter asked which other selection methods added the highest extra amounts of predictive power, assuming that a general intelligence test is already being used. The best was an integrity test, which added another 27 per cent to the predictive power. Giving a work sample or a structured interview would both add 24 per cent extra predictive power. Where these could be applied, it would be sensible to add one or more of these in addition to the general mental test. Using multiple methods is sensible in these cases, because it leads to even better decisions. Tests of the personality trait called conscientiousness and reference checks are also helpful additions to the general mental ability test.

In the setting of finding a bunch of people who will do a range of jobs better than just taking people at random, an intelligence test has utility. It will not predict anywhere near to perfectly how well people do a job. People will still hire workers who are not good at the job and with whom they can't get on. But, on the whole, it is better to include a general mental ability test in a portfolio of selection methods.

Frank Schmidt and John Hunter made additional useful points in a later, non-systematic review. The correlation between intelligence and performance in job training, based on 980 studies, is strong at all levels of job complexity, between 0.54 and 0.65. Their review of evidence refuted the idea that specific aptitudes might be better predictors of job training than general intelligence; general mental ability measures did better. A remarkable finding is that general intelligence predicts job performance just as well, if not slightly better, as job experience increases. They spent some of their review looking for a reason for the strong intelligence–job performance correlation and they conclude that an intervening factor is job knowledge: 'People who are higher in GMA [general mental ability] acquire more job knowledge and acquire it faster.' They ended their article with a conclusion as follows: 'Nearly 100 years ago, Spearman (1904) proposed that the construct of GMA is central to Human affairs. The research presented in this article supports his proposal in the world of work, an area of life critical to individuals, organizations, and the economy as a whole.'

Success in life beyond intelligence

In order to avoid an accusation of oversimplification, let me repeat that we all know it takes more than brains to be successful, and sometimes it does not take brains much at all. Returning to Sir Walter Scott's *Kenilworth*, the young Walter Raleigh knew that he could progress beyond older and less successful courtiers, due to some non-cognitive qualities: '"Why, sirs," answered the youth [Raleigh], "ye are like goodly land, which bears no crop because it is not quickened by manure; but I have that rising spirit in me which will make my poor faculties labour to keep pace with it. My ambition will keep my brain at work, I warrant thee."'

At the same time that we repeat and recognize that high intelligence is far from sufficient for success, there is some evidence that more success can accrue to those with ever-higher levels of intelligence. If one wants to find out how successful people are who, in youth, have eye-wateringly high levels of cognitive capability, then the work of David Lubinksi and Camilla Benbow is recommended. For example, after forty years, those who were in the top 1 per cent of the population for mathematical reasoning ability at age 13 years were, in middle age, more likely to be tenured academics at the best universities, top executives in Fortune 500 companies, and lawyers in the big firms. They had produced large numbers of books, research articles, and patents, and been successful in gaining research funding.

Intelligence predicts occupational and educational successes. That's 'wealthy and wise' covered. Next, let's see about 'healthy'.

Chapter 8
Does intelligence matter for health and longer life?

'Ultimate validity of psychological tests': that was a catchy title for an academic journal article that appeared in 1992. The authors were Brian O'Toole and Lazar Stankov. They examined data from Australian soldiers at the time of the Vietnam war. They concluded that 'a general intelligence test...is a good predictor of mid-life mortality'; in other words, the likelihood of having died by mid-life. For several decades, intelligence tests were used in education and in the workplace, as described in Chapter 7. This was different; might intelligence tests have some predictive power in health, and even for death? This new field is called cognitive epidemiology. For a comprehensive example from the field, let's look at how a whole population's intelligence, tested at age 11 years, was associated with how long they lived, up to sixty-eight years later.

The Scottish Mental Survey of 1947

Catherine Calvin headed this study of ours. It is the only follow-up of a near-complete population with regard to whether higher intelligence in childhood predicts longer life.

The Scottish Mental Survey of 1947 tested 70,805 children attending Scottish schools on Wednesday, 4 June 1947. All the children were born in 1936. They sat the Moray House Test No. 12 of general intelligence. They comprised about 94 per cent of the

Scottish children born in 1936. We tried to find out who among the 70,805 was still alive on 31 December 2015, when they would be 79 years old. For those who died, we tried to find out what they died of. We wanted to find out if their intelligence test score from age 11 years was related to surviving to age 79. We wanted to know whether childhood intelligence was related to some causes of death and not to others.

To answer these questions we had to link the data from the Scottish Mental Survey 1947 with health records. Remember that, at age 11, females' surnames might not be the same as those that appeared later in health records, owing to marriage. This was just one of the difficulties in trying to trace those 70,000+ children several decades later. With the permission of the Registrar General of Scotland, we asked National Records of Scotland to link the Scottish Mental Survey 1947 to medical records in the National Health Service Central Register in Scotland. Around 10 per cent of those Scottish schoolchildren moved to England and Wales in subsequent years. For completeness, we wanted to link their intelligence test scores to survival too. The MRIS Integrated Database and Administration System did the linkage to the NHS Central Register in England and Wales. Vital status—alive or dead—was recorded for all those who were traced. Cause of death was classified according to the International Classification of Diseases system. I have just summarized a linkage process that took my team about three years to accomplish.

Of the 70,805 children tested in the Scottish Mental Survey 1947, we traced 65,765 to health records as of 31 December 2015. Those who were alive would be 79 years old, and have lived for sixty-eight years after taking the Moray House Test No. 12 of general intelligence at age 11. The number traced is more than 92 per cent of the 1947 Survey's participants. The average time to follow-up was fifty-seven years; 25,979 had died, and 30,464 were still alive. There were 9,322 whose vital status was not known; this included people who had emigrated from Great Britain, people who had disappeared from medical records, and a few others.

There was a positive association between a higher intelligence test score at age 11 years on 4 June 1947 and the likelihood of being alive on 31 December 2015. Here is the result in simple numbers: on average, a child who had an advantage of 15 points on an IQ scale at age 11 had about a 20 per cent lower risk of being dead by age 79. The robustness of the result can be given as numbers which represent the 95 per cent confidence intervals; that is the range of values which are 95 per cent likely to contain the true value. Here, the 95 per cent confidence interval was 22 per cent to 19 per cent, meaning that the 20 per cent estimate was probably accurate.

That was the result for all causes of death lumped together. I shall next describe some specific causes of death, and how strongly they related to childhood intelligence test scores. Over 9,500 people died of cardiovascular disease. An advantage of 15 IQ points in intelligence at age 11 was associated with a 24 per cent lower risk of dying from cardiovascular disease by age 79 (95 per cent confidence interval was 25 per cent to 23 per cent).

Figure 21 shows the association between intelligence test score at age 11 and dying of cardiovascular disease by age 79. The intelligence test scores are divided into ten groups, from the lowest group to the highest. This is not how the analyses were done—they used all of the individuals' actual test scores—but the grouping is done here for illustration. Along the bottom is the number of each tenth of intelligence test score division. The lowest-scoring IQ group is called the reference group ('Ref'). Up the left-hand side is the risk of being dead from cardiovascular disease, called the hazard ratio. The hazard ratio of the lowest-scoring tenth is set arbitrarily to 1.0, so we can compare the other groups. Identify the left-most point on the graph. That is the Reference, lowest IQ group, who have a hazard ratio value of 1.0. Note that

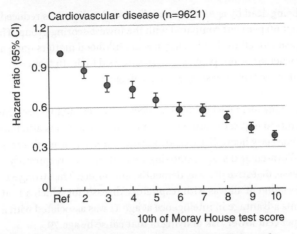

21. This is one of twelve diagrams in the report by Calvin et al. representing the association between intelligence test scores at age 11 and the likelihood of death from various causes up to sixty-nine years later. Along the bottom is the Moray House Test score of general intelligence divided into tenths; 'Ref' is the lowest scoring group and 10 is the highest; 9,621 people died of cardiovascular disease. Up the left-hand side, the hazard of the lowest-scoring Reference group is set at 1. Note the steady decline in risk with higher intelligence test scores. The top group has less than 40 per cent of the risk of the lowest-scoring group.

the other nine points to the right have T-shaped vertical extensions. These are 95 per cent confidence intervals. They are small, meaning that the estimates are robust. As one moves rightward from the Reference group, the hazard numbers decrease steadily. This is important; it tells us that, as the intelligence test score at age 11 becomes higher and higher, the risk of death from this cause by age 79 steadily lowers. The association between lower childhood intelligence and earlier death from cardiovascular disease is not confined to just the lower levels of intelligence test score. Even the second-highest-scoring intelligence group does less well than the highest-scoring group. Identify the right-most point on the graph. This is the highest-scoring childhood intelligence group. Their hazard is about 0.4; that is, their hazard of being dead by age 79 from cardiovascular disease is reduced by about 60 per cent compared with the lowest-scoring group. This appears to tell us that intelligence in childhood matters quite a lot for whether or not people have succumbed to death from cardiovascular disease by 79 years of age.

A steadily increased protective effect of higher intelligence, from lowest- to highest-scoring intelligence test group, was also found for coronary heart disease, stroke (these first two are subsets of cardiovascular disease), smoking-related cancers, respiratory disease, digestive disease, dementia, and injury. The strongest association of all was with respiratory disease, for which a 15 IQ points advantage in intelligence at age 11 was associated with a 28 per cent lower risk of dying of that cause by age 79 (95 per cent confidence interval, 30 per cent to 26 per cent). Compared with those in the lowest IQ tenth, the highest-scoring tenth had about a 70 per cent lower the risk of dying from respiratory disease by age 79. There was an association between lower childhood intelligence and death from suicide in men, but not in women. The only causes of death that were not related to childhood intelligence were non-smoking-related cancers.

When people hear about these strong and near-comprehensive— with respect to most major causes of death—findings, most then have a strong curiosity about why they occur. In this study, we had some participants who had information on socio-economic status in childhood, at the time of the intelligence testing. Adjusting for that made little difference to the results. That was not the explanation.

Our study also analysed another Scottish sample which had information on participants' socio-economic status in adulthood, and whether they were smokers. For some causes of death, adjusting for these factors reduced the association between intelligence and mortality between a quarter and almost two-thirds. However, for an advantage of 15 IQ-type points in intelligence, there was still a 23 per cent lower risk of dying from respiratory disease, and a 21 per cent lower risk of dying from coronary artery disease. Smoking and adult socio-economic status were, at best, only partially accounting for the intelligence–death associations. We also discussed the possible role of education, which, in other studies, can partially reduce the size of intelligence–death associations when it is taken into account. However, we thought that that is a moot point, because higher intelligence is associated with gaining more qualifications, as we saw in Chapter 7. Therefore, adjusting for education might, in effect, be partly adjusting for intelligence. Later on in this chapter, we shall think more about why higher intelligence from childhood might be associated with longevity, and be protective against early death from so many different causes.

Intelligence in youth and all-cause mortality

In a meta-analysis, also headed by Catherine Calvin, we had, prior to the study we just discussed, found sixteen studies that had reported associations between intelligence test scores in youth and deaths from all causes. All these studies were from general population cohorts. The studies took place in five countries: the United Kingdom (7), the USA (5), Sweden (2), Australia (1), and Denmark (1). The smallest study had 862 people in it. The largest was just short of a million people; it was a study of male Swedish conscripts. The intelligence tests came mostly from military conscription records or school testing. Intelligence was tested at between 7 years old and 20 years old. The studies were published between 1988 and 2009. In fact, fifteen of the sixteen appeared between 2001 and 2009. Overall, the sixteen studies included more than 1.1 million people, of whom over 22,000 had died. The follow-up periods ranged from seventeen to sixty-nine years.

The main result from this meta-analysis was that an advantage of 15 IQ points in youth was associated with a 24 per cent lower risk of death during the follow-up periods. The size of the association was similar in men and women. Because the Swedish conscripts study was so large, we re-computed the results after omitting that study; they didn't change. Childhood social advantage was not responsible for the intelligence–mortality association. Some studies had information on people's education and adult socio-economic status. Adjusting for those factors reduced the intelligence–mortality associations between a third and a half. However, we discussed the possibility that education and adult socio-economic status might reflect, to an extent, earlier intelligence level.

Let's sum up so far. There is a robust association between higher intelligence test scores in early life and living longer, and having a lower risk of dying from several causes. When we look at the next studies we shall also find that, on average, people with higher childhood intelligence have a lower risk of developing various illnesses and are more likely to adopt healthier behaviours as adults. All of this research—apart from the pioneering results from the Australian soldiers of the Vietnam War era—appeared in the 21st century.

In 2001, Lawrence Whalley and I reported the first study to find a link between higher childhood intelligence and longer life. It was based on a subset of the Scottish Mental Survey 1932. The size of the association between childhood intelligence and longevity was similar to that found in the larger studies described already. My reason for mentioning it is that our discussion in that 2001 report put forward four possible and non-exclusive causes for the link between childhood intelligence and health and longevity. They were as follows:

1. Intelligence test scores in childhood might be indicators of accumulated bodily insults to that age, and therefore be a partial index of departure from optimal health, overall.

2. High childhood intelligence test scores might represent a better-wired-together body, overall, from birth or even earlier; this idea was called 'system integrity'.

3. Higher childhood intelligence might lead to more education and subsequently to professional jobs; this might have health advantages, including entry into safer environments.

4. Higher childhood intelligence might be associated with the greater uptake of healthy behaviours and lifestyles.

Since our list was suggested in 2001, the major explicit addition has been the possibility that intelligence and health outcomes—including longevity—might have partially shared genetic contributions. We saw some evidence for that in Chapter 4, which recounted genetic correlations between intelligence and many health factors.

Part of the research in this field of cognitive epidemiology asks whether, in addition to longer life, higher intelligence is associated with lower risk of developing certain illnesses, and with adopting healthier behaviours. These outcomes are of interest in themselves. They are also interesting because they might help partly to explain the intelligence–death associations.

The National Longitudinal Survey of Youth 1979

This is one of our analyses, headed by Christina Wraw. The National Longitudinal Survey of Youth 1979 is a USA-based sample that had 12,686 participants. We met them in Chapter 3. They were representative of their age-group, which was 14 to 21 years old at the end of 1978. They were first tested in 1979. They provided data on health, social factors, employment, and attitudes. Up to 1994 they had an interview each year; after that, it was every two years. At the beginning of the study they took an intelligence test called the Armed Forces Qualifications Test. Its four subtests are arithmetic reasoning, mathematics knowledge, word knowledge, and paragraph comprehension.

The health data we analysed here were from their survey in 2012. There were results on more than 7,000 of the participants. Sixteen health conditions were assessed, drawn from the 'health module' that 5,793 of the participants completed when they were about 50 years old. Nine of these conditions were responses to being asked whether a doctor had ever diagnosed them with a given condition.

Higher intelligence test scores in youth were associated with a lower risk of being diagnosed with a number of common illnesses by about 50 years of age. The results are expressed here as the percentage lower risk of that diagnosis per 15 IQ points advantage in the intelligence test score. Higher intelligence in youth was associated with lower risk of being diagnosed by age 50 with: high blood pressure (20 per cent), diabetes (15 per cent), chronic lung disease (29 per cent), heart problems (21 per cent), congestive heart failure (34 per cent), stroke (35 per cent), and arthritis (16 per cent). Intelligence does not just relate to length of life; it is also related to the likelihood of being diagnosed with many illnesses by middle age.

Other health outcomes in our report came from self-reported questionnaires. Those survey participants with higher intelligence test scores in youth had better physical health and health status overall, and had fewer difficulties with mobility.

Adjusting for childhood socio-economic status had little influence on these results. Therefore, childhood deprivation was not an explanation for the intelligence–health associations. We also adjusted the results for people's adult socio-economic status, which was a combination of education, income, and occupational status. There were some large reductions of the intelligence–health associations when we took these factors into account. We discussed that this did not afford a single interpretation. It might be that any protective effect of early-life intelligence on health status in middle age is working via social advantages. It might also be that education, income, and occupational status are acting to an extent as a proxy for intelligence test scores. Of the individual indicators of adult socio-economic status, it appeared that relative poverty might partially explain the association between lower intelligence and poor health.

Christina Wraw and our team reported another two sets of results from the same National Longitudinal Survey of Youth 1979 dataset. In the first one, we looked at mental health at the age of 50 years. Participants with higher intelligence test scores in youth had less depression in middle age, as assessed with a standard questionnaire. They reported fewer problems with sleep. For a 15-IQ-points advantage in youth, there was a 22 per cent lower risk of reporting poor mental health at age 50. On the other hand, those with higher intelligence in youth were slightly more likely to report having had a diagnosis of depression at some point in their lives. We speculated that this latter result might arise from those with higher intelligence being more aware of the symptoms via better health literacy, and then seeking to have something done about it. Or, it might be to do with the health insurance situation in the USA, whereby one might need a diagnosis before having paid-for treatment. Once again, adjusting for childhood socio-economic status had little influence on the results, but adjusting for adult socio-economic status did reduce the intelligence–mental health associations considerably.

Christina Wraw headed our third report on the National Longitudinal Survey of Youth 1979. We tested associations between intelligence in youth and health behaviours at 50. On average, those with 15 IQ points' advantage in intelligence test score from youth were 40 per cent less likely to smoke at age 50, 33 per cent less likely to have had an alcohol drinking session in the last month at which they consumed six or more drinks, and were 47 per cent more likely to floss their teeth. I won't give all the numbers associated with them, but those with higher intelligence test scores in youth were also, at age 50: more able to do moderate cardiovascular activity and strength training; less likely to have had a sugary drink recently; and more likely to often read nutritional information on items when shopping.

I am sometimes asked about the implications of this area of research. A research-based answer is that it is good to find out why there are social inequalities in health, and to find that intelligence differences might have a part to play in that. A more pragmatic answer is that it might be a good idea to find out and copy what smart people do, health-wise, because they appear on average to live healthier and longer lives. There is overwhelming evidence that higher intelligence in youth is related to healthier behaviours in adulthood, lower risk of illnesses, and longer life. But there is much work to be done to find out why these associations exist.

Chapter 9
Is intelligence increasing generation after generation?

A person is 30 years old; the year is 1940. A psychologist measures their height with a ruler, and measures their intelligence with a well-known IQ test. Next, take another 30-year-old. This time, the year is 1970. Their height and intelligence are measured using the same ruler and the same IQ test. They both obtain the same height, and the same intelligence test score. Is the conclusion that these two people are the same height and of the same intelligence level? The former is probably correct, but the latter is probably wrong. The problem is something called the 'Flynn effect'.

The (James) Flynn effect of rising IQ

The key researcher here is James Flynn, a political scientist from the University of Otago, New Zealand. The first thing Flynn brought to serious scientific scrutiny was that mental test companies had to redo the norms for their scores every so often. This rather boring-sounding, technical problem is the source of one of the largest unexplained puzzles in the field of intelligence research. When a psychologist buys a mental test from a psychometric company, they receive the test questions and the answers, and instructions for giving the test in a standard way. The psychologist needs something else. A person's score on the test does not mean anything unless the psychologist has some indication of what is a low, high, and average score. Therefore, with the test, comes a booklet of normative scores, or 'norms'. This is a series of tables which indicate how any given score fits into the relevant population's scores. Usually they are divided for age, because some test scores change with age (Chapter 2). Therefore, the psychologist can find out how the person tested did when compared with their age peers. Usually the tables of norms indicate what percentage of the population would have scored higher or lower than the score of the person who was tested. Those of us who have measured our children's heights and compared them with the population average for their ages will be familiar with this type of referencing to norms.

James Flynn noticed that tables of norms for intelligence tests had to be changed every several years. As new generations came along, they were scoring too well on the tests, by comparison with people who were their age some years before. The tests seemed to be getting easier. A generation or two after the companies produced the tables of normative scores, the 'average' person of a given age in the later generation was scoring above the 'average' person of the same age in the earlier generation. For example, 20-somethings tested in the 1980s were doing better on the same test than 20-somethings from the 1950s. The norms were becoming outdated—Flynn called them 'obsolete'.

The response of the intelligence test companies to their tests' norms becoming out of date was to 're-norm' the tests. The norms tables were altered so that, as time went on, it became harder to achieve a score that got a person above any given percentage of their peers. For example, the same test score on the same test in, say, 1950 or 1970 would result in a higher IQ in 1950 than in 1970. It's worse than that. Let's say a person takes the test on the last day that the institution testing them used the old norms of the test. They take the test and obtain an IQ score. The tester looks up the norms tables and states that the person made the cut above some percentage of their age peers. If that same person had taken the same test on the first day of the new norms—just a day later—the same score would put them significantly further down the percentage of the population; they would obtain a lower IQ score. In fact, the test companies would not always alter the norms tables. The other manoeuvre they adopted was to make the test harder so that the person had to take a new, harder test to get to the same point on the population's scale, that is, the same IQ.

In summary, as the 20th century progressed, populations' scores on some well-known intelligence tests were improving when compared with same-age people generations earlier. Just as average height had increased over generations, people began to wonder if intelligence was rising.

Flynn published results in 1984 that gave IQ test-users an alarm call. 'Everyone knew' that tests had to be re-normed every so often, but Flynn quantified the effect and spelled out its consequences. He quantified the effect in a smart piece of psychological detective work. He searched for every study he could find in which groups of people had been given two different IQ tests for which the norms were collected at least six years apart. This is the key idea. Flynn asked: what would the sample's estimated IQs be when compared with the earlier and the later norms? For clarity, he decided to look exclusively at samples of white Americans. He found 73 studies, involving a total of 7,500 people, aged from 2 to 48 years. These studies included the Stanford–Binet and the Wechsler scales; these are among the most used and best-validated intelligence tests.

Flynn found that people's estimated IQs were higher when they were based on older norms, by contrast with more recent norms. On perusing all the samples he collected, the effect was fairly constant over the period from 1932 to 1978. During that time, white Americans gained more than 0.3 of an IQ point every year, about 14 IQ points over the epoch. Over the middle part of the 20th century, the American IQ rose by a large amount. Flynn warned that, 'If two Stanford–Binet or Wechsler tests were normed at different times, the later test can easily be 5 or 10 points more difficult than the earlier, and any researcher who has assumed the tests were of equivalent difficulty will have gone astray…. Allowing for obsolescence in intelligence testing is just as essential as allowing for inflation in economic analysis.' At the end of his first large-scale study on this topic, James Flynn came up with three points that might explain the 'massive gains' that successive American generations were attaining in IQ scores.

First, they might be an artefact. The gains might be 'not real, but an artefact of sampling error'. That is, the groups recruited to provide norms might, over time, become more biased toward containing cleverer people. This is unlikely to have occurred in such a systematic way as to make all later normative samples brighter than all earlier ones. Even if this is part or whole of the explanation, it still makes scores across older and newer versions of IQ tests non-comparable.

Second, they might be test sophistication. Successive generations might not actually be more intelligent. They might just be scoring better on the tests for some reason that we have to go and find. There might be some experiences, which change over time, that prepare people more optimally for sitting intelligence-type tests. Perhaps the tests' questions have leaked out.

Third, they might be a real intelligence increase. If the test score differences represent real increases in intelligence, they are hard to explain. Flynn tried to examine the most likely candidate: that socio-economic improvements accounted for the IQ gains across generations. However, he thought the gargantuan alterations that would be needed in living standards to account for all of the IQ changes were not plausible.

Flynn's 'Massive IQ gains in 14 nations'

In a review three years after his first one, James Flynn wanted more definitively to identify the source of the rising IQ scores.

Broadening out from the USA, he sought examples of IQ test scores that had been collected across generations. Here's how he described that search: 'The method used to collect data can be simply put. Questionnaires, letters, or personal appeals (usually a combination of all three) were sent to all those researchers known to be interested in IQ trends on the basis of scholarly correspondence and the exchange of publications. One-hundred sixty-five scholars from 35 countries were contacted.' Some of Flynn's strongest data came from military samples, in those countries where nearly all young men sat IQ tests at entry to compulsory military service. Figure 22 illustrates some of Flynn's data.

Here's how to look at Figure 22. The vertical scale at the left-hand side is an IQ scale. Along the top are some different countries from which Flynn obtained good data. In each country, the most recently available data have been set at an arbitrary IQ score of 100. These appear at the top of the five vertical lines. An IQ of 100 is, by an arbitrary definition, the population average. For each of the five countries in the figure, there was earlier testing of the same population. The dates down the dotted vertical lines show

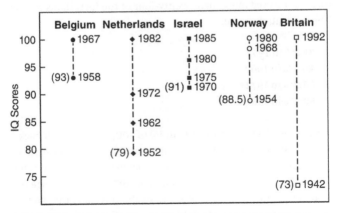

22. Generation by generation, many nations are scoring better on IQ-type tests.

how much lower the population's IQs were in earlier years of testing. Note the dots on each vertical line with a date against them: these dates are when the IQ testing of the population took place. Reading across from these dots/dates to the IQ score numbers on the extreme left shows what the average IQ of the population was at that date, compared with the 100 score of the most recently tested population. All of these occasions of testing should give rise to average IQs of 100. They do not. Whenever a population was tested at an earlier date, the imputed IQ average was lower. The effect that Flynn first found in American whites occurred in other countries. Flynn named his 1987 article 'Massive IQ gains in 14 nations'.

Take the example of the Netherlands. Since 1945, the Dutch military have tested almost all young men in the Netherlands on forty of the sixty items of Raven's Progressive Matrices. Because this testing exercise is population wide, there is almost no worry here about testing cleverer-biased samples in later years. Raven's Matrices is a non-verbal mental ability test of abstract reasoning, and is supposed to be quite good at testing general intelligence. Flynn examined these data and reported the percentage of young men who scored more than twenty-four of the forty items correct. The percentages were:

31.2% in 1952
46.4% in 1962
63.2% in 1972
82.2% in 1981/2.

Setting the 1982 scores to a mean IQ of 100, one can work back and ask the question: what was the mean IQ score of the earlier generations based on the percentage that achieved the pass rates? Figure 22 reveals that the Dutch men in 1972 had an average IQ of about 90, the 1962 population were about 85, and the 1952 population were below 80. Additional proof of this increase arose from a comparison of over 2,800 men tested in 1981/2 with their fathers tested in 1954. The sons were 18 IQ points higher than their fathers who had been tested 27½ years earlier. Therefore, we see this puzzling effect even in people who are genetically related and who have lived in the same culture, where we would expect similar average IQ scores.

In Figure 22, Norwegian data for approximately the same period show gains for later generations too, but they are smaller than those of the Dutch. Belgian military data showed a rise of 7 IQ points over the relatively short period from 1958 to 1967. New Zealand children gained an average of 7.7 IQ points between 1936 and 1968 (data not shown). Two further sets of data from Flynn's large number of comparisons are shown: Israeli people gained 11 IQ points over the fifteen years from 1970 to 1985. People in the United Kingdom went from a mean IQ of 73 in 1942, to 100 in 1992.

That UK increase makes a good illustration of the impact if these changes were real alterations in intelligence levels. Compared with a mean of 100 in 1992, the mean for the population in 1942 would be almost at a level that indicated significant learning disability for the average person. That makes me sceptical about the possibility of these IQ score gains reflecting better brain power.

Let's summarize from Flynn's data on samples from fourteen nations. For a generation (thirty years) he found IQ gains between 5 and 25 points, with an average of 15. These data are stunning findings of some cultural shifts in intelligence tests' scores, and challenging for researchers in the field of intelligence.

A surprise within the 'Flynn effect' of rising IQ scores is that the biggest effects tend to occur in so-called culturally reduced tests. IQs rise most markedly in those tests whose items can't easily be learned. For example, Raven's Progressive Matrices is among the tests that show the highest gains over generations. Yet, Raven's Matrices involves finding the correct answer that completes an abstract pattern. It has no words, no numbers, nothing really that can be taught so that the later generation will do better than the former. Flynn's review of his massive datasets confirmed this:

> A consensus about the significance of generational IQ gains depends, therefore, on whether they manifest themselves on culturally reduced tests like the Raven's. These tests maximise problem-solving and minimise the need for more specific skills and familiarity with words and symbols. [There are] strong data for massive gains on culturally reduced tests: Belgium, the Netherlands, Norway, and Edmonton show gains ranging from 7 to 20 points over periods from 9 to 30 years; when the rates of gain are multiplied by 30 years, they suggest that the current generation has gained 12–24 points on this kind of test. Tentative data from other nations are in full agreement. This settles the question at issue: IQ gains since 1950 reflect a massive increase in problem-solving ability and not merely an increased body of learned content.

The Flynn effect is well established. Its importance is reflected in the eponymous title, and in the interest it has attracted since the late 1980s. The American Psychological Association had a full meeting on the issue, and published a book in which many experts sought an answer to it. It is easy, and accurate, to summarize by saying that the experts were dumbfounded. There are two broad responses to the Flynn effect.

The first response is to suggest that the Flynn effect is real, marking an actual improvement in brain power in successive generations across the 20th century. People who opt for this account suggest that we have a good exemplar in height. Human height has increased across the century, probably as a result of better nutrition and general health, so why not intelligence? Flynn did not favour this option. He worked out that, in countries such as the Netherlands and France, where there have been high IQ gains across generations, teachers should now be faced with classes in which 25 per cent are gifted and where geniuses have increased sixtyfold: 'The result should be a cultural renaissance too great to be overlooked.' Flynn searched French and Dutch newspapers, especially periodicals relating to education, from the late 1960s to the present, and found no mention of any great increase in intellectual achievements by newer generations.

The second response suggests that the Flynn effect is an artefact. This states that it is not the case that people are more intelligent. Instead, what has happened is that people have become more familiar with the mental tests' materials. Children's toys, magazines, games, television programmes, and so forth might contain materials that have IQ-item-like properties, and so people do better on the tests when they come across them. The Flynn effect occurred largely before computers were used in daily life; therefore, that is not the cause of the rise in intelligence test scores.

Flynn emphasized the following about his effect: it does not compromise the validity of mental test scores within generations. Mental test scores, despite the 'massive gains' through time, retain their reliability, their ability to predict educational and job successes, but only within each generation. The Flynn effect does not compromise the genetic contributions to intelligence test scores, as discussed in Chapter 4. Similarly, height retained its high heritability despite population increases in its average. The key point is that something in the environment or culture of many countries across the middle years of the 20th century has led to cognitive ability test scores increasing substantially. Many researchers think that it has to be the environment because some of the across-generation samples tested fathers and sons.

Flynn made a telling point when he asked us to reflect on the fact that being born a generation or so apart can make a difference of 15 IQ points. We have no good account of the causes for this change; it is officially mysterious. Given that he could find no evidence for the present generation's genius in achievement over former generations, Flynn's opinion was that IQ tests like Raven's do not measure intelligence, but only some correlate of intelligence, which he called 'abstract problem-solving ability'. Further, he insisted that differences in this ability are 15 points between successive generations, and these differences must arise from some environmental factor. He concluded that IQ test differences cannot be used to make trustworthy comparisons of the intelligence of different generations or of different cultural groups. Perhaps most importantly of all, he pointed out that, because IQ score was one criterion for whether or not a convicted murderer could be executed in the USA, the Flynn effect could be a matter of life or death.

'One century of global IQ gains'

Flynn's papers from 1984 and 1987 are classics, with monumental amounts of work in them. They alerted intelligence researchers to a large problem, and have stimulated much research and thinking. Yet, Flynn's data were indicative—and, I think, convincing—rather than systematic and definitive. They did not form a meta-analysis, and probably not even a systematic review. Jakob Pietschnig and Martin Voracek conducted a meta-analysis of the Flynn effect.

They systematically searched the scientific literature and found 219 relevant studies on the Flynn effect. There were 271 separate samples with a total of almost four million people. The samples were from thirty-one countries, from Africa, Asia, Australasia, Europe, and North and South America. Participants had been tested as long ago as 1909, and as recently as 2013, that is, a period of more than a century. Seventy per cent of the samples' participants were younger than 17 years old when tested, and 90 per cent were under 40 years old. Almost 70 per cent were samples of healthy people. I won't go into all the details, but there were five types of study design that allowed them to test for Flynn effects. The first two were: using the same intelligence test on two demographically similar groups in different years; and giving a sample of people the original and a revised version of the same test.

Figure 23 shows Pietschnig's and Voracek's results. Along the bottom are the years in which the mental testing was done. Up the left-hand side are the changes in IQ scores as time moves on. There is a line for general 'full-scale' IQ, and lines for fluid and crystallized IQs that were described in Chapter 2. There is a line for spatial IQ. The scores of the earliest year available for each type of IQ are set to a baseline of zero. By looking at a year, tracing one's finger up to a given line, and then tracing the finger over to the left, one can see by how much IQ has risen by that year. Before doing that, just notice that the lines go up from the bottom left to the top right. Flynn was right: around the world, intelligence test scores of later generations are higher than those of earlier ones. The century looked at here shows a rise of 20 to 30 points; as Flynn wrote, decades ago, these are massive gains.

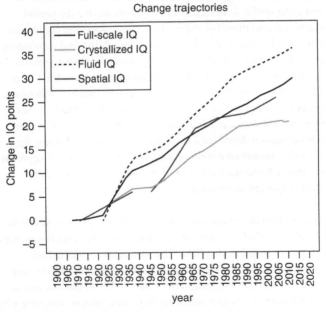

23. **Rises in IQ scores by types of intelligence test, from 1909 to 2013.**

Pietschnig and Voracek found an average rise in IQ of 2.8 points every ten years. There was a greater rise for fluid intelligence (4.1 points per decade) than crystallized intelligence (2.1 points per decade). Matrices tests (see Figure 2) are an example of a 'fluid IQ' type test. Vocabulary tests are a type of crystallized test. They thought they detected a slowing down of the IQ gains during the Second World War, which they thought might be partly due to relatively poor nutrition in some countries. They detected a slowing down of the IQ gains in the most recent decades, from the 1970s.

They spent a long time discussing possible causes of the Flynn effect. They explored whether their data could help to decide which causes were more plausible. They found few convincing data. They thought there was some evidence that people's having more years of full-time education and better educational systems might explain some of the effect. They realized that computers and other media were largely not available during the period examined, and therefore exposure to technology that could train thinking skills was not a likely cause. They didn't find convincing evidence that the reduction in family sizes over time contributed much. They were quite keen on the idea that some of the Flynn effect might be explained by later generations' greater willingness to guess on certain types of intelligence test. Other factors that they thought might partly account for later generations' higher IQs included reduced lead exposure (from paint and water, for example), improved nutrition, and less pathogen stress (e.g. from infectious diseases). Background improvements in economic prosperity were mentioned.

Another idea that Pietschnig and Voracek considered was one of Flynn's own, that he came up with some years after his discoveries. It is called social multipliers. The idea is that small initial advantages in ability—perhaps affected by genetic differences, perhaps by better environments—lead to better performance, which in turn leads to a better environment. That is, someone who performs well on something might be 'spotted' as good and be given, or opt for, extra tuition and practice, perhaps with better materials and circumstances than others. Thus, better environment causes positive increments in performance, which in turn begets even better environments. And so on: it multiplies. Small initial advantages might multiply into huge performance differences later on via these feedback loops. This might happen on a whole-society scale if societies decide to focus more on cognitive performance. There has been no direct test of this idea.

Most of these ideas—there were at least twelve of them—about possible causes of the Flynn effect end up with the same conclusions: they probably explain, at best, only part of the effect; there is little direct evidence for them; and they are hard to prove or test. Pietschnig and Voracek appreciated that some of the causes might have come to saturation, which might account for the reported levelling-off of the Flynn effect recently, for example in Norwegian data.

I thought two comments made toward the end of Pietschnig's and Voracek's long article were worth repeating. I think that some of the Flynn effect is not real. As these authors put it, 'the question remains whether the portion of IQ gains that cannot be explained by guessing [or other forms of test sophistication etc.] in fact reflects meaningful gains'. And this: 'it would be difficult to argue that the present IQ increase of about 30 points over the past century means that the average person born in the early 1900s had in fact an adjusted IQ of 70 and was therefore according to our present classifications learning disabled'.

I think the Flynn effect is about as mysterious in origin(s) as it ever was, though the evidence for its existence is better. The reader might like to reflect on the Flynn effect and its causes, not least because some fresh thinking on this matter might offer psychologists a foothold on a slippery problem. If there were a prize in the field of human intelligence research, it might be for the person who can explain the 'Flynn effect' of the 'rising IQ'.

Chapter 10
Do psychologists agree about intelligence differences?

As an interested layperson, it is not easy to sift the well-validated facts about human intelligence differences. Some commentators in the area represent one extreme or the other in advocating IQ testing. Media coverage often reflects this, putting one side of the debate, or just the two extremes, or merely reporting the slanging match. It took a furore to knock some heads together and for psychologists to appreciate that there was a broad consensus about many research findings on human intelligence. The resulting report by the American Psychological Association (APA) was one of the most useful accounts of intelligence research to become available for the non-specialist. The report is about a quarter of a century old at the time of this writing, and most of it is still correct, and a good primer.

The Bell Curve

We'll come to that APA report. First, here's the furore. In the mid-1990s, a book called *The Bell Curve* (Figure 24) by Richard Herrnstein (who died in the same month that the book was published) and Charles Murray rewrote the rules for academic book distribution. Almost 900 pages long, almost 300 of which were statistical analyses, detailed footnotes, and academic journal references, it sold hundreds of thousands of copies in the USA. It

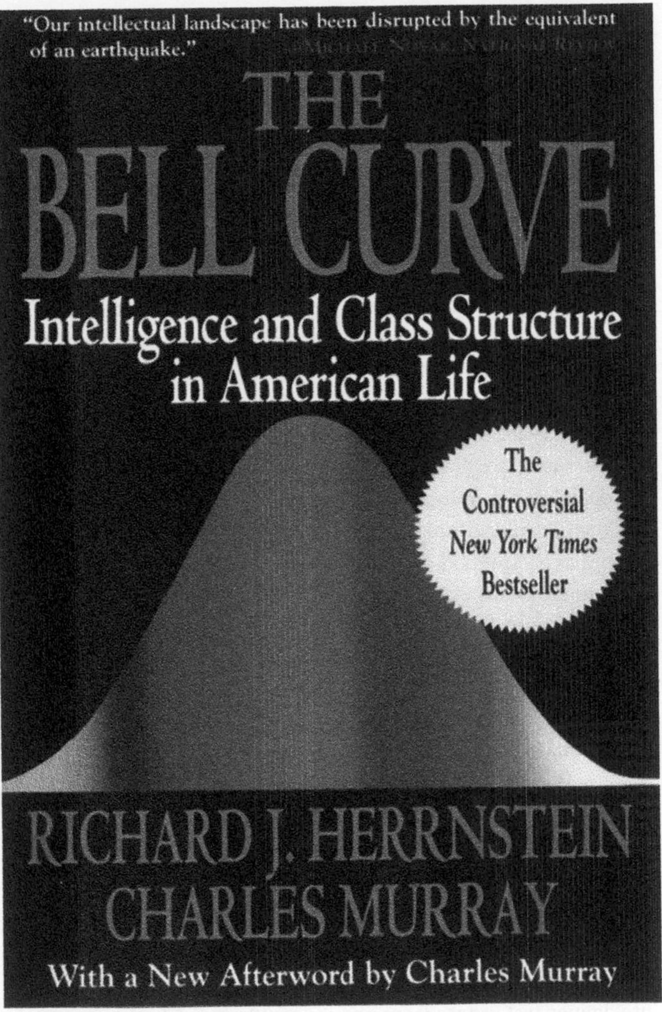

24. The cover of *The Bell Curve*.

brought most disputes concerning human intelligence differences freshly to the pages of newspapers and magazines. It provoked the Western world (at least) and the psychological research community into a turmoil over the impact that mental ability differences have on people's destinies. The book presumed to address IQ scores in the context of predicting social outcomes and social policies. One especially controversial part of the book was on ethnic differences. The resulting controversy alerted the professional psychological associations: if people were arguing about intelligence differences, shouldn't they be provided with some largely undisputed facts as a basis for commenting on *The Bell Curve*'s contents?

I read *The Bell Curve* in the middle of its initial firestorm. The book is a mixture of reviews of past literature on intelligence and social policy, many novel empirical analyses of the National Longitudinal Survey of Youth 1979 (we saw this sample in Chapters 3 and 8), and social policy opinions and recommendations. Although it had proved to be an unexpectedly successful way to make money, I thought it was a missed academic opportunity. In part II (pages 127 to 266 in my edition) of *The Bell Curve*—'Cognitive classes and social behavior'—there was a series of analyses on only non-Hispanic white people from the 1979 Survey. Herrnstein and Murray examined the associations between intelligence test scores taken in young adulthood (late teens to very early twenties) and the following social outcomes by their early thirties: poverty, schooling, unemployment, injury, family matters, welfare dependency, parenting, crime, and civility and citizenship. They also tested whether intelligence test scores were stronger predictors of these life outcomes than parental socio-economic status. Thus, they were asking: do higher intelligence test scores from about age 20 predict better educational outcomes, higher social position, and arguably more pro-social behaviours in the thirties? The answer was: they did. They then asked if this was due to (confounded by) parental socio-economic status; it mostly wasn't.

My opinion was these analyses in part II should have been reported in a scientific journal. The results were important, and they deserved to go via the rigour of peer review. That might have prevented their being lost in the reaction to the book, which involved many books and articles—lay and scientific—criticizing the work. However, the fact that I think Herrnstein's and Murray's part II results should have been published via another route does not mean that *The Bell Curve*'s authors presented the results of part II badly. One will rarely see such fully and clearly described and well-illustrated statistical analyses. At the end of the book, there is a thirty-page appendix with their output of the statistical analyses of part II, just in case one wants to check them. Thus, these authors went to unusual lengths to show their workings and to describe their analyses and results accessibly. I still recommend having a look at part II of *The Bell Curve*.

This recommendation notwithstanding, anyone's trying to say, 'Have a look at part II of the Bell Curve. There are some interesting analyses about whether or not intelligence predicts important life outcomes', would have been like trying to whisper 'shush' to the crowd during the last eight seconds of the first quarter at Arrowhead Stadium, Kansas City, on 29 September 2014. If Herrnstein and Murray had published the part II analyses in a peer-reviewed scientific journal, it might have afforded those results more positive critical notice rather than being lost in the controversy following the book's appearance. But they didn't, and we may resort to the proverb that it's an ill wind that blows nobody any good, because there was at least one good response to the controversy.

A working party on intelligence's knowns and unknowns

Here's that response. The American Psychological Association decided that they had a responsibility to put on record some findings about human intelligence differences that attracted broad consensus among psychologists. Their Board of Scientific Affairs (BSA) appointed a Task Force to collect what researchers did and did not know about human intelligence differences. My aim in this chapter is to show that the report from this Task Force is a still-useful and mostly unbiased summary of the topic. It adds variations to the themes raised in this book and is a good source of further reading.

The APA Task Force's report comprehensively and concisely told the wider world what is and what is not known about human intelligence (IQ) differences. Here's how they introduced their report:

> In the fall of 1994, the publication of Herrnstein and Murray's book *The Bell Curve* sparked a new round of debate about the meaning of intelligence test scores and the nature of intelligence. The debate was characterised by strong assertions as well as strong feelings. Unfortunately, those assertions often revealed serious misunderstandings of what has (and has not) been demonstrated by scientific research in this field. Although a great deal is now known, the issues remain complex and in many cases still unresolved. Another unfortunate aspect of the debate was that many participants made little effort to distinguish scientific issues from political ones. Research findings were often assessed not so much on their merits or their scientific standing [see my points, above, about part II of the book] as on their supposed political implications. In such a climate, individuals who wish to make their own judgements find it hard to know what to believe.

The late Ulric Neisser, then Professor of Psychology at Emory University, was appointed to the chair of the Task Force. Other members were chosen by an extended consultative process, with the aim of representing a broad range of expertise and opinion. They included nominees from the APA Board on the Advancement of Psychology in the Public Interest, the Committee on Psychological Tests and Assessment, and the Council of Representatives. Disputes were resolved by discussion. The final report had the unanimous support of the entire Task Force.

It is difficult to overestimate the importance of this Task Force for wider communication about the study and understanding of human intelligence differences. Ulric Neisser was one of the best-known research psychologists in the world. He was the father of 'cognitive psychology', which is the area of psychology that studies mental processes. Much respected, he had not previously been associated with intelligence testing, and one assumes he was disinterested with respect to the topic. The range of experts on the panel might have been expected to argue vigorously and acrimoniously rather than to agree. There were well-known researchers from the field of the genetic–environmental studies of intelligence (Thomas Bouchard and John Loehlin), and from the more environmental approach (Stephen Ceci). There were people who took a broader view of intelligence: for example, Nathan Brody, who had dispassionately summarized the area of intelligence differences for fellow academics in a book. There was Robert Sternberg, whose theories of intelligence differences go far beyond, and sometimes disagree with, the typical conceptions of mental ability as encapsulated in IQ tests. There were representatives from the USA's Educational Testing Service (Gwyneth Boodoo) and people with an interest in the education of minority groups (A. Wade Boykin), in differences between the sexes (Diane Halpern), and in testing as applied to occupational outcomes (Robert Perloff). This was the world's arguably most influential psychological association bringing some respected and disparately opinioned heads together and mandating them to produce a clear, unanimous statement about some knowns and unknowns of human intelligence differences.

There now follows a guide to the contents of the Task Force's report: I have indicated where it picks up issues raised in this book. The APA report does not put the reader in touch with actual studies and data, as I have done in this book, but it provides a complementary resource for facts about intelligence differences.

The APA Task Force on conceptions of intelligence

The first topic the Task Force addressed was the key question of what psychologists mean when they study intelligence. They agreed that the word covered many aspects of mental working and their relative efficiency but that, 'When two dozen prominent theorists were recently asked to define intelligence, they gave two dozen somewhat different definitions...Such disagreements are not cause for dismay. Scientific research rarely begins with fully agreed definitions, though it may lead to them.'

They did recognize that the main conception of intelligence differences was encapsulated in the so-called psychometric approach. Psychometric means measurement applied to aspects of the mind. That is the approach covered in this book, and is the research field that is associated with the idea of intelligence testing and the scores they produce. As we saw in Chapter 1, tests of mental measurement cover a wide range of mental capabilities. In addition, though, the APA Task Force recognized that there were conceptions of intelligence that emphasize aspects of mental ability not covered by typical IQ-type tests. To repeat, what is tested by mental ability (intelligence) tests is by no means all that human brains are capable of. The Task Force report discussed a wide range of conceptions of intelligence that attempt to go beyond an IQ-type view of mental abilities.

The APA Task Force on intelligence tests and their correlates

This next section of the Task Force's report asked whether mental test scores relate to anything else. A scientist might measure some aspect of mental functioning and find that some people score better than others: however, in all honesty, she cannot claim that the test scores derive from some prior definition of intelligence. Unlike height or blood pressure, there is no scale from zero to whatever. The measurements of mental ability do not reflect known aspects of the brain's functioning. The cognitive tasks involved in the intelligence tests might appear to be measuring the efficiency of some types of mental effort, but why should one be interested in them? For three reasons, perhaps.

First, if differences in mental test scores are substantially stable through people's lives, then some partly consistent aspect of human mental capability has been reckoned. This was covered in Chapter 2 in this book, and the Task Force report usefully summarizes other supportive research in this area.

Second, if mental tests' scores can contribute towards the prediction of some aspects of human life that are independent of the test materials, then they have significance that is wider than their surface content. The areas of life to which mental tests are often applied are work, school, and clinic. These issues are often to do with mental tests' capacity to act as a convenient aid to selection and prediction. The APA Task Force report discussed the associations between intelligence test scores and school performance, years of education, job performance, and broader social outcomes such as crime and delinquency. Some of these associations—education and selection in the workplace—were described in Chapter 7 of this book. At the time of the Task Force's writing, cognitive epidemiology had not begun, and there was almost no appreciation, then, of intelligence test scores' associations with health outcomes and mortality; see my Chapter 8.

Third, there is another aspect of correlates of intelligence test scores to do with where the differences in scores come from. That is, can we discover anything about the brain's performance that relates to mental test score differences? If this were possible, and if some of the differences in mental test scores were related to aspects of brain processing, then we would be in a better position to understand how the differences in brains produce differences in mental ability. The APA Task Force's report discussed how intelligence test scores correlate with components of cognition, reaction time, inspection time, and aspects of neurological function. In Chapters 5 and 6 I introduced some of these supposedly simpler aspects of brain function and structure and their associations with mental test scores.

The APA Task Force on genetic and environmental contributions to intelligence

The APA Task Force's report considered the evidence for genetic and environmental contributions to intelligence differences. Their report goes into more detail and covers more individual twin and adoption studies and topics than I did, though it was composed before DNA-based GWAS studies had been conceived or were possible (Chapter 4). With regard to the environment, the Task Force agreed that one of the most intriguing findings to emerge in recent years is the generation-upon-generation rise in IQ test scores known as the Flynn effect (discussed here in Chapter 9).

The APA Task Force on group differences in intelligence

The last topic that the APA Task Force addressed was group differences in intelligence. These 'groups' were based upon the sexes and ethnic groups. I described some sex differences in Chapter 2. I recommend reading the Task Force's treatment of the controversial issue of ethnic differences, which was one of the main topics that caused the stramash over *The Bell Curve*.

The APA Task Force's conclusions

I end this summary of the APA Task Force's report by listing some of the topics that its members thought remained unanswered or mysterious about human intelligence, despite almost a century of research. Here, according to the Task Force's report, are some of intelligence researchers' unknowns. They were presented as some challenges for future research.

1. There is some influence of genes on intelligence, but its exact nature is unknown.

2. The aspects of the environment that affect intelligence are unknown.

3. It is not clear how nutrition affects intelligence.

4. It is not known why intelligence test scores correlate with simpler measures of human performance (see my Chapter 5).

5. There is no satisfactory explanation of why intelligence test scores are increasing with successive generations.

6. The reasons for intelligence test score differences between various groups are not known.

7. There is too little known about the important human abilities that are not tested by intelligence tests (creativity, wisdom, practical sense, social sensitivity).

Many years on from the APA Task Force's report, we know a bit more about 1 (but not enough), and the rest of these unknowns are still unknown.

Summaries of intelligence research after the APA Task Force

As a follow-up to the APA's task force report, I recommend an article by Richard Nisbett and colleagues. It did not have the same selection process for the panellists. These authors are more often associated with criticisms of intelligence testing, and with interests in the more environmental contributions to intelligence differences. However, they cover much interesting research and, despite what I just said, they say this quite near the start of their piece:

The measurement of intelligence is one of psychology's greatest achievements and one of its most controversial. Critics complain that no single test can capture the complexity of human intelligence, all measurement is imperfect, no single measure is completely free from cultural bias, and there is the potential for misuse of scores on tests of intelligence. There is some merit to all these criticisms. But we would counter that the measurement of intelligence—which has been done primarily by IQ tests—has utilitarian value because it is a reasonably good predictor of grades at school, performance at work, and many other aspects of success in life... intelligence test scores remain useful when applied in a thoughtful and transparent manner.

There is coverage of the environmental contributions to intelligence differences. For example, they discuss whether breast feeding enhances a child's intelligence. This issue is difficult to settle, because some studies have found that a proportion of any slight association between breast feeding and the child's intelligence is due to (confounded by) the mother's intelligence test score. To be clear, some studies suggest that higher-intelligence-test-scoring women have higher-intelligence-test-scoring children and also happen to be more likely to breast-feed them. The issue is not settled. There are other good reasons to breast-feed babies; it is not certain, though, that it will boost their IQs. Nisbett referred to interesting results finding that the adoption of children into more socially advantaged homes is associated with boosts to intelligence test scores. There is a discussion of how more education can boost intelligence.

I think the Nisbett report is less authoritative and less even-handed than the Neisser one. However, it provides an update on many of the topics discussed in the APA's Task Force report, and offers views worth airing on many aspects of intelligence research. I would suggest that the reader partners it with my own survey of intelligence research in the *Annual Review of Psychology*, from the same year. It is a complement rather than an alternative to

Nisbett's report. It covers many of the topics in this book, and has many more references to individual studies.

Signing off, and encouragement to read more...

Well, I hope some of my 'ten quite interesting things about intelligence test scores' were interesting. One of the reasons I took my solid-findings-up-front-based approach is that I do not think it is optimal to start with the historical controversies about intelligence and crawl toward some emerging decent findings. That's a common approach, but I don't think it is helpful for an introduction to what we know about the topic from more recent data; the APA task force took a similar view. The history of intelligence and intelligence testing are interesting and sometimes salutary. I have written about some historical aspects of intelligence, such as processing speed. However, one may amass useful knowledge about intelligence and its differences from good modern data without having first to trudge through intelligence's past. But do go and find out more about the latter; I offer a guide at the end of the 'Further reading' section.

As I wrote at the start of the book, I haven't tried to cover everything. Especially, I haven't tried to cover topics for which the research overall is poor (say, creativity, or wisdom), where the data are often of the straw-in-the-wind variety (say, functional brain imaging, or attempts to boost intelligence [good luck with that]), or where my judgement is that they are interesting but not really about human intelligence differences (say, emotional intelligence or artificial intelligence).

Arming the reader with good data and accumulated results on my ten topics isn't my final aim. One sign of a good book is that, when you close it, you want to open more books and articles on the same topic. Therefore, at the end of this *Very Short Introduction*, an 'introduction', remember, I offer a guide to wider reading on intelligence. There are recommendations for more topics, and more on the topics that I addressed. I am happy to point to different opinions, though do always ask how good the data are that lie behind them.

Appendix
A word about correlation

The use of statistics is central to research on how and why people differ in intelligence test scores. Researchers typically test large numbers of people on a variety of tests of thinking. Discovering the pattern of differences between people, and how they relate to things in real life, cannot be done without statistical examination of the data. Some of the key debates in human intelligence are about statistical matters. Worse still, the statistical techniques we employ in intelligence research are among the more complicated ones in the discipline of psychology. There was no point in trying to fashion a wee book on intelligence that bristled with statistics: no one would read it. In the end, I decided that there was no escaping one type of statistic: correlation.

Correlation is a way of describing how closely two things relate to each other. It is expressed as a number called a correlation coefficient. The range of values that a correlation coefficient can take is from –1, through 0, to 1.

Here's an example. Imagine that I stop the first 100 adult women whom I meet in the street and measure their heights and weights. I want to know whether being taller also means being heavier. I calculate a correlation coefficient using a formula. It will tell me how strongly the heights and weights are related. Imagine that everyone who was taller than someone else was also heavier than them. There would be a perfect association between the two: the correlation would be 1. That does not happen in real life. We all know some short fat people and some tall thin people. Generally, the taller people are heavier, but there are many exceptions. Therefore, there is a strong trend toward taller people weighing more, but it is not perfect. The correlation is probably around 0.5, which is a highish positive correlation.

Extend that example. Imagine that I also decided to measure the length of their hair. I am curious to know whether the taller people grow their hair longer. I am almost certain that there is no tendency for tall people to have their hair either longer or shorter than smaller people. My guess is that height would have no association with hair length at all. If I am correct, the correlation coefficient would be 0. The two things would have no tendency to go together.

Here's one more extension to the example. Let's say that, in addition to measuring people's heights, we ask them to walk a measured distance, say 20 metres. We count the number of steps it takes them. I am curious to know whether there is any association between height and the number of steps it takes to cross this distance. My guess is that taller people would tend to take fewer strides. The correlation coefficient would probably confirm this; but, notice that it would find that being taller would go along with taking a smaller number of steps. Therefore, the correlation would be negative; as one value (height) goes up, the other one (steps taken to cover 20 metres) goes down. I guess it might be about −0.4. However, the value is not the important thing here. The point I want to make is that correlations can have negative or positive values. It's when the value of the correlation is zero that there is no relationship between two things. In summary: a correlation can describe for us whether one thing tends to go up or down with another thing, or whether there is no relation at all between the two.

Next, we need to have a word about the sizes of correlations. I mentioned above that height and weight probably had a fairly high correlation, about 0.5 or thereabouts, or maybe more. In fact, I got the 0.5 value by calculating it from heights and weights of a number of real people's data. In psychology and other sciences that look at social phenomena, we do not often find correlations beyond about the 0.5 level. There is a convention that correlation coefficients above about 0.5 are called large or strong effects. Those between about 0.2 and 0.5 are called medium, modest, or moderate. Those below 0.2 are called small or weak.

For variety, I shall not always refer to correlations between two things. Sometimes I shall say the 'relation' or the 'relationship', and at other times I shall say the 'association'. When I use these words I am referring to a correlation. And if I qualify any of these terms with the adjectives large, medium, or small, these will refer to the sizes of coefficient mentioned in the previous paragraph.

In science there is a mantra that goes, 'correlation does not imply causation'. It is worth remembering. It prevents our making simplistic inferences about what causes what. However, correlations do have causes. Therefore, when I present correlations in this book I shall attempt to offer a fair range of possible reasons for them. In intelligence research, there are many correlations, but few of them have adequate causal accounts. We know a lot about what goes with what, but rarely why.

People sometimes make the common error of applying the correlation to themselves, personally. Let's say we announce that we have tested heights and weights of people and we say that there is a strong correlation, such that taller people tend to be heavier. A short, portly person might well look at themselves and exclaim that we are talking nonsense, that they are living proof that there's no such association. We must recall that, in any situation where a correlation is not +1 or −1 (i.e. almost all the time), we shall find exceptions to the association. The lower the correlation, the more exceptions we shall find when we meet individual people. Moreover, finding a correlation in one group of people does not guarantee that we shall find the same association in other samples of people.

Here's another, general warning: intelligence test scores might have some associations with things in life, but there is always a lot more to any human story than just intelligence. Intelligence is never all that matters.

Three words about meta-analysis: replication, replication, replication

It is a good rule not to trust any single study on a topic. Throughout the book I aim to present large and well-designed studies to illustrate key topics in intelligence research. However, it is also a good idea to ask if other studies give the same results. In science, findings should be replicated when the same topic is studied using the same methods. It is good scientific practice to ask what the results are like when one puts together all the studies in a field of research. Doing this is called a systematic review; this is where a scientist or team will scour the published—and often the unpublished, too—international scientific literature to find all reports that address the same question.

Going a stage beyond the systematic review is a meta-analysis. That is where the results of all available studies are put onto the same scale, and the reviewer tries to express the overall, average finding. Sometimes that's expressed as a correlation. For example, imagine that someone wanted to know whether there was an association between people's heights and weights. I argue that they should not trust the single result I presented above. They could search for all studies in which height and weight were measured on groups of people. Then, they could list the correlations obtained by all the studies and work out the average correlation.

That's a meta-analysis. They might also give more influence to larger than to smaller studies, and get a weighted-average correlation. To explain, imagine that three studies used the same methods to test the heights and weights of different people, and that one study tested a thousand people, another one tested a hundred people, and the third one tested ten people. It is a good idea to let the larger study have more influence on what is reckoned to be the average correlation.

There are problems with meta-analyses. For example, they often contain a mix of good and not-so-good studies. Therefore, true effects can be diluted or obscured. As much as the reviewer tries to select studies addressing the same topic, they almost always end up with a list of reports that do things in at least slightly different ways, resulting in the 'comparing apples and pears' objection. These objections and others notwithstanding, I think it is useful to know whether there is a meta-analysis for a given question, and what it suggests as a crude bottom line for the result. If, say, every study looking at the correlation between intelligence test scores and brain size found approximately the same result, or not, that is worth knowing.

In the book's chapters, I often follow up a good illustrative single study with the results of a meta-analysis on the same topic.

References and further reading

Below, I refer to the main studies described in each chapter, and
 sometimes an additional accessible source on the same topic.

Here are some other people's broad accounts of intelligence:

Mackintosh, N. J. (2011). *IQ and Human Intelligence*, 2nd edition.
 Oxford: Oxford University Press.

Ritchie, S. J. (2015). *Intelligence: All That Matters*. London: John
 Murray Learning.

Sternberg, R. J. (ed.) (2019). *Human Intelligence: An Introduction*.
 Cambridge: Cambridge University Press.

Chapter 1: Is there one intelligence or many?

Here are the main studies I mentioned:

Carroll, J. B. (1993). *Human Cognitive Abilities: A Survey of Factor
 Analytic Studies*. Cambridge: Cambridge University Press.

Gardner, H. (1983, reissued 1993). *Frames of Mind: The Theory of
 Multiple Intelligences*. New York: Basic Books.

Gardner, H. (1999). *Intelligence Reframed: Multiple Intelligences for
 the 21st Century*. New York: Basic Books.

Warne, R. T., & Burningham, C. (2019). Spearman's g found in 31
 non-western nations: strong evidence that g is a universal
 phenomenon. *Psychological Bulletin*, 145, 237–72.

Wechsler, D. (2008). *Manual for the Wechsler Adult Intelligence
 Scale-Fourth Edition (WAIS-IV)*. San Antonio, Tex.: Pearson.

Chapter 2: What happens to intelligence as we grow older?

Here are the main studies I mentioned:

Corley, J., Cox, S. R., & Deary, I. J. (2018). Healthy cognitive ageing in the Lothian Birth Cohort studies: marginal gains not magic bullet. *Psychological Medicine*, 48, 187–207.

Deary, I. J. (2014). The stability of intelligence from childhood to old age. *Current Directions in Psychological Science*, 23, 239–45.

Plassman, B. L., Williams, J. W., Burke, J. R., Holsinger, T., & Benjamin, S. (2010). Systematic review: factors associated with risk for and possible prevention of cognitive decline in later life. *Annals of Internal Medicine*, 153, 182–93.

Salthouse, T. A. (2009). Selective review of cognitive ageing. *Journal of the International Neuropsychological Society*, 16, 754–60.

Tucker-Drob, E. M., Brandmaier, A. M., & Lindenberger, U. (2019). Coupled cognitive changes in adulthood: a meta-analysis. *Psychological Bulletin*, 145, 273–301.

Here's a useful book and a useful overview article:

Salthouse, T. A. (2010). *Major Issues in Cognitive Ageing*. Oxford: Oxford University Press.

Tucker-Drob, E. M. (2019). Cognitive aging and dementia: a life-span perspective. *Annual Review of Developmental Psychology*, 1, 7.1–7.20.

Chapter 3: Are there sex differences in intelligence?

Here are the main studies I mentioned:

Deary, I. J., Irwing, P., Der, G., & Bates, T. C. (2007). Brother–sister differences in the *g* factor in intelligence: analysis of full, opposite-sex siblings from the NLSY1979. *Intelligence*, 35, 451–6.

Deary, I. J., Thorpe, G., Wilson, V., Starr, J. M., & Whalley, L. J. (2003). Population sex differences in IQ at age 11: the Scottish Mental Survey 1932. *Intelligence*, 31, 533–42.

Strand, S., Deary, I. J., & Smith, P. (2006). Sex differences in cognitive ability test score: a UK national picture. *British Journal of Educational Psychology*, 76, 463–80.

Here's a useful book:

Halpern, D. (2011). *Sex Differences in Cognitive Abilities*, 4th edition. London: Routledge.

Intelligence

Chapter 4: What are the contributions of environments and genes to intelligence differences?

Here are the main studies I mentioned:

Davies, G., 218 authors, & Deary, I. J. (2018). Study of 300,486 individuals identifies 148 independent genetic loci influencing general cognitive function. *Nature Communications*, 9, 2098.

Haworth, C. M. A., 22 authors, & Plomin, R. (2010). The heritability of general cognitive ability increases linearly from childhood to young adulthood. *Molecular Psychiatry*, 15, 1112–20.

Reuben, A., Caspi, A., Belsky, D. W., Broadbent, J., Harrington, H., Sugden, K., Houts, R. M., Ramrakha, S., Poulton, R., & Moffitt, T. E. (2017). Association of childhood blood lead levels with cognitive function and socioeconomic status at age 38 years with IQ change and socioeconomic mobility between childhood and adulthood. *Journal of the American Medical Association*, 317, 1244–51.

Here's a useful book:

Plomin, R. (2018). *Blueprint: How DNA Makes Us Who We Are*. London: Allen Lane.

Chapter 5: Are smarter people faster?

Here are the main studies I mentioned:

Deary, I. J., Johnson, W., & Starr, J. M. (2010). Are processing speed tasks biomarkers of cognitive ageing? *Psychology and Aging*, 25, 219–28.

Der, G., & Deary, I. J. (2017). The relationship between intelligence and reaction time varies with age: results from three representative narrow-age cohorts at 30, 50 and 69 years. *Intelligence*, 64, 89–97.

Here's a useful lay overview:

Deary, I. J., & Ritchie, S. J. (2014). Ten quick questions about processing speed. *British Academy Review*, 24, Summer. It is available free, here: <http://www.thebritishacademy.ac.uk/10-quick-questions-about-processing-speed.>

Chapter 6: What do more intelligent brains look like?

Here are the main studies I mentioned:

Cox, S. R., Ritchie, S. J., Fawns-Ritchie, C., Tucker-Drob, E. M., & Deary, I. J. (2019). Structural brain imaging correlates of general intelligence in UK Biobank. *Intelligence*, 76, 101376.

Gignac, G. E., & Bates, T. C. (2017). Brain volume and intelligence: the moderating role of intelligence. *Intelligence*, 64, 18–29.

Haier, R. J. (2016). *The Neuroscience of Intelligence*. Cambridge: Cambridge University Press.

Pietschnig, J., Penke, L., Wicherts, J. M., Zeiler, M., & Voracek, M. (2015). Meta-analysis of associations between human brain volume and intelligence differences: how strong are they and what do they mean? *Neuroscience and Biobehavioral Reviews*, 57, 411–32.

Ritchie, S. J., Booth, T., Valdes Hernandez, M. C., Corley, J., Munoz Maniega, S., Gow, A. J., Royle, N. A., Pattie, A., Karama, S., Starr, J. M., Bastin, M. E., Wardlaw, J. M., & Deary, I. J. (2015). Beyond a bigger brain: multivariable brain imaging and intelligence. *Intelligence*, 51, 47–56.

Chapter 7: Does intelligence matter in the school and the workplace?

Here are the main studies I mentioned:

Deary, I. J., Strand, S., Smith, P., & Fernandes, C. (2007). Intelligence and educational achievement. *Intelligence*, 35, 13–21.

Lubinski, D., Benbow, C. P., & Kell, H. J. (2014). Life paths and accomplishments of mathematically precocious males and females four decades later. *Psychological Science*, 25, 2217–32.

Schmidt, F. L. (2016). The validity and utility of selection methods in personnel psychology: practical and theoretical implications of 100 years of research findings. It is available by request from here: <https://www.researchgate.net/publication/309203898>.

Schmidt, F. L. & Hunter, J. E. (1998). The validity and utility of selection methods in personnel psychology: practical and theoretical implications of 85 years of research findings. *Psychological Bulletin*, 124, 262–74.

Schmidt, F. L. & Hunter, J. (2004). General mental ability in the world of work: occupational attainment and job performance. *Journal of Personality and Social Psychology*, 86, 162–73.

Here's a useful review article:

Strenze, T. (2007). Intelligence and socioeconomic success: a meta-analytic review of longitudinal studies. *Intelligence*, 35, 401–26.

Chapter 8: Does intelligence matter for health and longer life?

Here are the main studies I mentioned:

Calvin, C. M., Batty, G. D., Der, G., Brett, C. E., Taylor, A., Pattie, A., Cukic, I., & Deary, I. J. (2017). Childhood intelligence in relation to major causes of death in a 68 year follow-up: prospective population study. *British Medical Journal*, 357, j2708.

Calvin, C. M., Deary, I. J., Fenton, C., Roberts, B. A., Der, G., Leckenby, N., & Batty, G. D. (2011). Intelligence in youth and all-cause mortality: systematic review and meta-analysis. *International Journal of Epidemiology*, 40, 626–44.

Wraw, C., Deary, I. J., Der, G., & Gale, C. R. (2016). Intelligence in youth and mental health at age 50. *Intelligence*, 58, 69-79.

Wraw, C., Deary, I. J., Gale, C. R., & Der, G. (2015). Intelligence in youth and health at age 50. *Intelligence*, 53, 23-32.

Wraw, C., Gale, C. R., Der, G., & Deary, I. J. (2018). Intelligence in youth and health behaviours in middle age. *Intelligence*, 69, 71-86.

Chapter 9: Is intelligence increasing generation after generation?

Here are the main studies I mentioned:

Flynn, J. R. (1984). The mean IQ of Americans: massive gains 1932 to 1978. *Psychological Bulletin*, 95, 29-51.

Flynn, J. R. (1987). Massive IQ gains in 14 nations: what IQ tests really measure. *Psychological Bulletin*, 95, 29-51.

Pietschnig, J. & Voracek, M. (2015). One century of global IQ gains: a formal meta-analysis of the Flynn effect. *Perspectives on Psychological Science*, 10, 282-306.

Chapter 10: Do psychologists agree about intelligence differences?

Here are the main studies I mentioned:

Deary, I. J. (2012). Intelligence. *Annual Review of Psychology*, 63, 453-82.

Herrnstein, R. J. & Murray, C. (1994). *The Bell Curve*. New York: Free Press.

Neisser, U., Boodoo, G., Bouchard, T. J., Boykin, A. W., Brody, N., Ceci, S. J., Halpern, D. F., Loehlin, J. C., Perloff, R., Sternberg, R. J., &

Urbina, S. (1996). Intelligence: knowns and unknowns. *American Psychologist*, 51, 77–101.

Nisbett, R. E., Aronson, J., Blair, C., Dickens, W., Flynn, J., Halpern, D. F., & Turkheimer, E. (2012). Intelligence: new findings and theoretical developments. *American Psychologist*, 67, 130–59.

Some historical reading on intelligence

Research on human intelligence differences has an interesting history. The word controversy recurs, in relation to whether or not there is a *g* factor, whether it declines with age, whether it relates to brain structure, the relative importance of environments and genetics, group differences, school selection, alleged fraudulent results, and so forth. I encourage some reading about its history.

One book to note is Charles Spearman's *The Abilities of Man*. This is his big book on *g*, the statistical regularity he discovered in 1904 and that has been replicated for well over 100 years. There is history, empirical work, and theory in this book; and there are lots of ideas about intelligence. There are statements about group differences that are offensive to read. There is also Spearman's strong writing voice. As I hear it, he is often annoyed and arguing against an obtuse, misguided opponent. I can't think of anyone else who would have an early sub-section (p. 11) of a chapter entitled 'THE WORD "INTELLIGENCE" CANKERED WITH EQUIVOCALITY.

Another book to note is Francis Galton's *Hereditary Genius*. It may be obtained as a free pdf from the Francis Galton website. Beware: Galton invented the word eugenics. There are statements in the book about group differences and eugenics that are offensive to read. Before there were scientific studies on intelligence, Galton was about the first to conceive the idea of general mental ability, to suggest that it might be normally distributed in the population, to suggest that it might be substantially heritable, and to theorize about its foundations in simpler psychological processes. Galton has some unusual ways of putting things. For example, in explaining his idea of general mental ability—the idea that if a person is good at one mental skill they tend to be good at others, too—he argues against those who have the contrary notion of people having specialized skills, 'They might just as well say that, because a youth had fallen desperately in love with a brunette, he could not possibly have fallen in love with a blonde. He may or may not have more natural liking for the former type of beauty than the latter, but it is as probable as not the affair was mainly or wholly due to a general amorousness of disposition' (p. 24). There are a few hundred pages in the centre of the book which contain his empirical work; they are dry family assemblies of genius.

The big three historical figures in the history of intelligence are typically Galton, Spearman, and Alfred Binet. Binet invented the first intelligence tests. In the place of something specifically on Binet, I recommend Leila Zenderland's book. It gives a thriller of a story about how Binet's intelligence test almost never made it to the USA, and the fast and over-zealous use/misuse of it when it did.

For an attention-holding series of stories of the many men (yes, all men) involved in the early days of intelligence testing, and the various controversies, I recommend Raymond Fancher's book.

Arthur Jensen's book is 700 pages of whack-a-mole-ing of objections to intelligence testing and the concept of general intelligence. It might have been called, 'There is not much *Bias in Mental Testing*'.

Because someone else will mention it to you anyway, I will list Stephen Jay Gould's book. It gets the psychometrics wrong, it is wrong on brain size and intelligence, and it is written with strong anti-IQ-testing bias.

Because I have used several of our results from follow-up studies of the Scottish Mental Surveys, I have recommended my book with Whalley and Starr, because it described the surveys' origins, organization, and early findings in more detail.

Deary, I. J., Whalley, L. J., & Starr, J. M. (2009). *A Lifetime of Intelligence: Follow-Up Studies of the Scottish Mental Surveys of 1932 and 1947*. Washington, DC: American Psychological Association.

Fancher, R. E. (1987). *The Intelligence Men: Makers of the IQ Controversy*. New York: Norton.

Galton, F. (1869). *Hereditary Genius: An Inquiry Into its Laws and Consequences*. London: Macmillan and Co.

Gould, S. J. (1996). *The Mismeasure Of Man: Revised and Expanded Edition*. New York: Norton.

Jensen, A. R. (1980). *Bias in Mental Testing*. London: Methuen.

Spearman, C. (1927). *The Abilities of Man: Their Nature and Measurement*. London: Macmillan and Co.

Zenderland, L. (2001). *Measuring Minds: Henry Herbert Goddard and the Origins of American Intelligence Testing*. Cambridge: Cambridge University Press.

Defining intelligence, at last

The American Psychological Association's Task Force (Chapter 10) wrote that definitions come at the end of research rather than the start. I agree, and therefore I waited until here before offering one. Many people repeat Linda Gottfredson's definition: 'Intelligence is a very general mental capability that, among other things, involves the ability to reason, plan, solve problems, think abstractly, comprehend complex ideas, learn quickly and learn from experience. It is not merely book learning, a narrow academic skill, or test-taking smarts. Rather, it reflects a broader and deeper capability for comprehending our surroundings—"catching on", "making sense" of things, or "figuring out" what to do.'

Gottfredson, L. S. (1997). Mainstream science on intelligence: an editorial with 52 signatories, history, and bibliography. *Intelligence*, 24, 13–23.

Index

For the benefit of digital users, indexed terms that span two pages (e.g., 52–53) may, on occasion, appear on only one of those pages.

Intelligence

CONSCIENCE
A Very Short Introduction
Paul Strohm

In the West conscience has been relied upon for two thousand years as a judgement that distinguishes right from wrong. It has effortlessly moved through every period division and timeline between the ancient, medieval, and modern. The Romans identified it, the early Christians appropriated it, and Reformation Protestants and loyal Catholics relied upon its advice and admonition. Today it is embraced with equal conviction by non-religious and religious alike. Considering its deep historical roots and exploring what it has meant to successive generations, Paul Strohm highlights why this particularly European concept deserves its reputation as 'one of the prouder Western contributions to human rights and human dignity throughout the world.

www.oup.com/vsi

FORENSIC PSYCHOLOGY
A Very Short Introduction
David Canter

Lie detection, offender profiling, jury selection, insanity in
the law, predicting the risk of re-offending, the minds of serial
killers and many other topics that fill news and fiction are all
aspects of the rapidly developing area of scientific psychology
broadly known as Forensic Psychology. *Forensic Psychology:
A Very Short Introduction* discusses all the aspects of psychology
that are relevant to the legal and criminal process as a whole.
It includes explanations of criminal behaviour and criminality,
including the role of mental disorder in crime, and discusses
how forensic psychology contributes to helping investigate
the crime and catching the perpetrators.

www.oup.com/vsi

THE LAWS OF THERMODYNAMICS
A Very Short Introduction
Peter Atkins

From the sudden expansion of a cloud of gas or the cooling of a hot metal, to the unfolding of a thought in our minds and even the course of life itself, everything is governed by the four Laws of Thermodynamics. These laws specify the nature of 'energy' and 'temperature', and are soon revealed to reach out and define the arrow of time itself: why things change and why death must come. In this *Very Short Introduction* Peter Atkins explains the basis and deeper implications of each law, highlighting their relevance in everyday examples. Using the minimum of mathematics, he introduces concepts such as entropy, free energy, and to the brink and beyond of the absolute zero temperature. These are not merely abstract ideas: they govern our lives.

> 'It takes not only a great writer but a great scientist with a lifetime's experience to explains such a notoriously tricky area with absolute economy and precision, not to mention humour.'
>
> **Books of the Year, Observer.**

www.oup.com/vsi

AUTISM
A Very Short Introduction
Uta Frith

This *Very Short Introduction* offers a clear statement on what is currently known about autism and Asperger syndrome. Explaining the vast array of different conditions that hide behind these two labels, and looking at symptoms from the full spectrum of autistic disorders, it explores the possible causes for the apparent rise in autism and also evaluates the links with neuroscience, psychology, brain development, genetics, and environmental causes including MMR and Thimerosal. This short, authoritative, and accessible book also explores the psychology behind social impairment and savantism and sheds light on what it is like to live inside the mind of the sufferer.

SLEEP
A Very Short Introduction
Russell G. Foster & Steven W. Lockley

Why do we need sleep? What happens when we don't get enough? From the biology and psychology of sleep and the history of sleep in science, art, and literature; to the impact of a 24/7 society and the role of society in causing sleep disruption, this *Very Short Introduction* addresses the biological and psychological aspects of sleep, providing a basic understanding of what sleep is and how it is measured, looking at sleep through the human lifespan and the causes and consequences of major sleep disorders. Russell G. Foster and Steven W. Lockley go on to consider the impact of modern society, examining the relationship between sleep and work hours, and the impact of our modern lifestyle.

BEAUTY
A Very Short Introduction
Roger Scruton

In this *Very Short Introduction* the renowned philosopher Roger Scruton explores the concept of beauty, asking what makes an object - either in art, in nature, or the human form - beautiful, and examining how we can compare differing judgements of beauty when it is evident all around us that our tastes vary so widely. Is there a right judgement to be made about beauty? Is it right to say there is more beauty in a classical temple than a concrete office block, more in a Rembrandt than in last year's Turner Prize winner? Forthright and thought-provoking, and as accessible as it is intellectually rigorous, this introduction to the philosophy of beauty draws conclusions that some may find controversial, but, as Scruton shows, help us to find greater sense of meaning in the beautiful objects that fill our lives.

A fascinating book, which I heartily recommend.

Brya Wilson, Readers Digest

www.oup.com/vsi

ONLINE CATALOGUE
A Very Short Introduction

Our online catalogue is designed to make it easy to find your ideal Very Short Introduction. View the entire collection by subject area, watch author videos, read sample chapters, and download reading guides.

http://fds.oup.com/www.oup.co.uk/general/vsi/index.html

SOCIAL MEDIA
Very Short Introduction

Join our community
www.oup.com/vsi

- Join us online at the official Very Short Introductions **Facebook** page.
- Access the thoughts and musings of our authors with our online **blog**.
- Sign up for our monthly **e-newsletter** to receive information on all new titles publishing that month.
- Browse the full range of Very Short Introductions online.
- Read **extracts** from the Introductions for free.
- Visit our library of **Reading Guides**. These guides, written by our expert authors will help you to question again, why you think what you think.
- If you are a teacher or lecturer you can order inspection copies quickly and simply via our website.